Kingdom Warfare

An Unveiled Look Into The Spiritual Realm

Written by: Tim Gregory, Ph.D.

Table Of Contents

Introduction

Kingdom Warfare takes a biblical look at the war we are engaged in as part of the Church of Jesus Christ with Satan and his dark kingdom. It is a war played out in the spiritual realm, and manifested in the physical one around us. It is also a war that goes ignored, for the most part, by a large portion of the body of Christ. Yet, it is a war that affects everyone.

Much of the Church would prefer to stay ignorant to the realities of the war between the Kingdom of our Lord and the kingdom of darkness. Fully aware of the Church's ignorance, Satan and his demonic horde have laid waste to unredeemed mankind who go about trapped in spiritual blindness, and much of the Church as well! We, as the followers of Christ are called to wage war against the forces of darkness! We are to be vigilant, refusing to turn a blind eye to the works of the enemy at play on this planet, engaging him on the field of battle just as our Lord did when He lived in a body of flesh! For the Scriptures declare, *"And you know that God anointed Jesus of Nazareth with the Holy Spirit and with power. Then Jesus went around doing good and healing all who were oppressed by the devil, for God was with him"* (Acts 10:38, NLT).

Charles H. Kraft said, *"We are involved in the battle. Jesus enlisted us to fight taking territory away from the evil one."* The Church of Christ, spread out across all denominations and nationalities, has been enlisted into the army of the Lord! And just as every army has an enemy and a war to fight, so do we! Our enemy will not be ignored, for their longing is the destruction of mankind and the theft of their eternal souls!

Jesus has enlisted you into His army! He has entrusted you with His work to redeem the souls of mankind back to God, while at the same time destroying all the lying works of the devil upon planet Earth, and standing firm for the sake of your family and loved ones against the wiles of the enemy!

Throughout this book you'll gain a more complete understanding of the enemy you are facing, and the war you are to be engaged in. You will also gain a better understating of how to successfully wage war against the forces of darkness!

May this book serve as a sounding alarm for you! Prepare yourself for battle! The enemy is upon us! Put on the full armor of the God, and unsheathe your blade! Be bold and fearless! The victory belongs to our Lord!

Chapter 1

Two Kingdoms

"For he has rescued us from the kingdom of darkness and transferred us into the Kingdom of his dear Son, who purchased our freedom and forgave our sins. Christ is the visible image of the invisible God. He existed before anything was created and is supreme over all creation, for through him God created everything in the heavenly realms and on earth. He made the things we can see and the things we can't see— such as thrones, kingdoms, rulers, and authorities in the unseen world. Everything was created through him and for him." Colossians 1:13-16 (NLT)

The Scriptures paint a clear picture of two kingdoms at war, the kingdom of our Lord, which is a kingdom of light, and the kingdom of darkness. Our Lord said He was the light of the world, and that light still shines today through His followers. On the other side is the kingdom of Satan, the archenemy of our Lord and of all that is good. His kingdom is one of darkness, made up of evil spiritual beings who have rebelled against our God, and a demonic horde that brings havoc and destruction to the children of men. And even though Jesus has overcome the world and toppled the spiritual forces of darkness, the fight continues, and will continue until Jesus returns.

To understand this war that rages on today, we must better understand the rebellions that have taken place in the spiritual realm against our Lord. Throughout this chapter we're going to look at three separate rebellions and how those rebellions have served to shape the world we live in today. We'll look at some familiar passages of Scriptures, and examine some other passages through a clearer lens, passages that are often quickly read through and given little thought. The first of these three rebellions involve Satan, the archenemy of God.

Satan's Rebellion

"Then there was war in heaven. Michael and his angels fought against the dragon and his angels. And the dragon lost the battle, and he and his angels were forced out of heaven. This great dragon—the ancient serpent called the devil, or Satan, the one deceiving the whole world—was thrown down to the earth with all his angels." Revelation 12:7-9 (NLT)

The Book of Revelation paints a clear picture of Satan's rebellion, and the outcome of that rebellion. The archenemy of God that we refer to as Satan today, was once a glorious angelic being who was given privileged access to the throne room of God. The Scriptures speak of his original state, saying, *"You were anointed as a guardian cherub, for so I ordained you. You were on the holy mount of God; you walked among the fiery stones"* (Ezekiel 28:14, NIV). As a cherub angel, Satan's original position would have been that of a throne room guardian, which would have made him a very powerful member of God's council. The Bible goes on to say he was blameless in all his ways, until one day iniquity was found in him. The iniquity caused him to desire the very throne he was charged with protecting; Satan wanted to take God's place. Pride was somehow birthed in Satan's heart, and as pride always does, it brought him to a great fall. The Prophet Isaiah also speaks of Satan's desire, and failure, to seize the Lord's throne when he writes, *"You said in your heart, I will ascend*

*to the heavens; I will raise my throne above the stars of God;
I will sit enthroned on the mount of assembly...I will ascend
above the tops of the clouds; I will make myself like the Most
High.*" *But you are brought down to the realm of the dead, to
the depths of the pit*" (Isaiah 14:13-15, NIV). Satan, the
original rebel, lost his place of authority and beauty, and was
cast down to the realm of the dead, where he hoped to keep all
of mankind as well, having led them to sin against God.

When Adam and Eve sinned, they lost their place of authority
in the physical realm, just as Satan had lost his place of
authority in the spiritual realm. When God created Adam and
Eve, He intended for them to represent Him, having authority
over all the earth, saying, "*Let us make humankind in our
image, according to our likeness; and let them have dominion
over the fish of the sea, and over the birds of the air, and over
the cattle, and over all the wild animals of the earth, and over
every creeping thing that creeps upon the earth*" (Genesis 1:26,
NRSV). And so, God created mankind with a specific purpose
in mind, the Scriptures further record God telling Adam and
Eve, "*Be fruitful and multiply, and fill the earth and subdue it;
and have dominion over the fish of the sea and over the birds
of the air and over every living thing that moves upon the
earth*" (Genesis 1:28, NRSV). God wanted mankind to have
dominion on earth, and to subdue it, keeping everything in-line
with the will of its Creator. As Satan and his rebellious angels
were part of God's family in the spiritual world, created to
serve His divine purpose, so Adam and Eve were part of God's
family in the physical world and were called to represent the
interest of their Creator.

When Adam and Eve rebelled against God, death and sin
entered the world, and now all would have to die and

experience eternal separation from the One who had created them, but God had plans that His archenemy didn't understand. As a cherub guardian and part of God's heavenly host, Satan was privileged to know a lot of God's workings, as did the other spirits who rebelled against God, but the Lord hadn't trusted them with everything, He understood with free will came the potential to rebel. The Book of Job tells us, *"God puts no trust even in his holy ones, and the heavens are not clean in his sight"* (Job 15:15, NRSV).

At the perfect time, God enacted His eternal plan to make a way for all of mankind to come back to Him of their own free will, when He sent Jesus Christ to die in our place, and raised Him to life again. The Scriptures say, *"Because God's children are human beings—made of flesh and blood—the Son also became flesh and blood. For only as a human being could he die, and only by dying could he break the power of the devil, who had the power of death. Only in this way could he set free all who have lived their lives as slaves to the fear of dying"* (Hebrews 2:14-15, NLT). Through Jesus Christ, God has taken the power of death away from the Satan, making a way for all those who trust in Christ to escape eternal judgement in the realm of the dead. Although Satan was the original rebel who led mankind away from God, bringing sin and death to the world, he would not be the last rebel, nor would he be the only spiritual being to bring chaos and decay to the world of man.

The Watcher's Rebellion

"In those days, and for some time after, giant Nephilites lived on the earth, for whenever the sons of God had intercourse with women, they gave birth to children who became the heroes and famous warriors of ancient times." Genesis 6:4 (NLT)

A lesser-known story of spiritual beings rebelling against their Creator is the story of the Watchers. This story is found in the sixth chapter of Genesis and tells of the sons of God leaving their natural state to have sexual relations with the daughters of men. The sons of God language is used to describe God's family in the spiritual realm and can be found in passages throughout the Bible, such as the Book of Job, when God speaks to Job about the formation of the earth, telling Job, *"To what were its foundations fastened? Or who laid its cornerstone, When the morning stars sang together, And all the sons of God shouted for joy"* (Job 38:6-7, NKJV)? In the beginning, when God created the earth, He had already created the spiritual host of Heaven, that is the sons of God.

Both Peter and Jude refer to this rebellion, speaking of the punishment rendered by God for their great trespass, for these sons of God had transgressed the boundary between the spiritual and physical realm, and would pay a hefty price. Peter writes, *"For God did not spare even the angels who sinned. He threw them into hell, in gloomy pits of darkness, where they are being held until the day of judgment"* (2 Peter 2:4, NLT). Jude writes, *"And I remind you of the angels who did not stay within the limits of authority God gave them but left the place where they belonged. God has kept them securely chained in prisons of darkness, waiting for the great day of judgment*" (Jude 1:6, NLT).

Now, besides Peter and Jude, none of the other New Testament writers speak of this rebellion, but there are other Second Temple sources that speak of this rebellion. These sources are not canonical, meaning they are not divinely inspired, but serve more as historical literature that testifies to the events, shedding historical light on the details of the rebellion. Two of these sources were found among the Dead Sea Scrolls, the Book of Enoch and the Book of Giants. They are both referred to as Second Temple writings because they were in use and written during the time of the Second Temple period, meaning the writers of the New Testament would have been very familiar with them, and some of them even referenced these Second Temple writings. These writings would have influenced the way the Jews of Jesus's day understood the world they lived in, especially the supernatural world, which is the unseen heavenly realm that Paul speaks of. Jude directly references the Book of Enoch when he writes, "*It was also about these that Enoch, in the seventh generation from Adam, prophesied, saying, 'See, the Lord is coming with ten thousands of his holy ones, to execute judgment on all, and to convict everyone of all the deeds of ungodliness that they have committed in such an ungodly way, and of all the harsh things that ungodly sinners have spoken against him*'" (Jude 1:14-15, NRSV). Jude uses this direct quote from the first Book of Enoch, known as the Book of Watchers, to clarify to his readers what the Day of the Lord will look like. Peter indirectly references the Book of Enoch when he speaks about the angels who sinned in 2 Peter 2:4, for although he does not say, "*the Book of Enoch says*" it is indeed a reference taken from the Book of Enoch that is found in no other Old Testament passage. So, we can see that even though some of these Second Temple Jewish writings are not canonical they can certainly help us to better understand some of the historical events that took place in ancient times, such as the Watcher's Rebellion and the consequences it brought upon mankind.

The phrase *watcher* does appear in the Old Testament, in the Book of Daniel, and a quick examination of that passage can help us to better understand the authority God has entrusted to them. In the fourth chapter of Daniel, we read of a dream King Nebuchadnezzar had of a judgment being passed on him because of his prideful attitude and refusal to give God the glory for the great kingdom He had blessed Nebuchadnezzar with. When Nebuchadnezzar tells Daniel of his dream (which Daniel interpreted for him) he says, "*I continued looking, in the visions of my head as I lay in bed, and there was a holy* **watcher***, coming down from heaven. He cried aloud and said: 'Cut down the tree and chop off its branches, strip off its foliage and scatter its fruit. Let the animals flee from beneath it and the birds from its branches. But leave its stump and roots in the ground, with a band of iron and bronze, in the tender grass of the field. Let him be bathed with the dew of heaven, and let his lot be with the animals of the field in the grass of the earth. Let his mind be changed from that of a human, and let the mind of an animal be given to him. And let seven times pass over him. The sentence is rendered by decree of the* **watchers***, the decision is given by* **order of the holy ones***, in order that all who live may know that the Most High is sovereign over the kingdom of mortals; he gives it to whom he will and sets over it the lowliest of human beings*'" (Daniel 4:13-17, NRSV).

9

Did you catch that? This account of Nebuchadnezzar's judgment is not remarkable because of what happens to him, but because the judgment was rendered by a decree from the Watchers. God himself didn't render the judgment, but rather a council of spiritual beings whom the Lord has entrusted with power and authority to represent Him. We see from this account that this group of spiritual beings, the order of the holy ones, has been given authority by God to make judgments on His behalf. That's a lot of power! From this Scriptural account we can see how powerful these beings are. The Book of Enoch tells of a group of these Watchers who rebelled against God, referred to as the sons of God in Genesis chapter six. Two hundred of them descended to the summit of Mount Hermon and swore an oath with each other to take for themselves wives of the daughters of men, and beget children with them (Enoch 1(6)2-6). Not only did these Watchers transgress the boundaries between the spiritual world and physical world by taking earthly wives for themselves, but they also taught mankind forbidden knowledge. They taught men how to make weapons of war from the metals of the ground, how to do enchantments, astrology, and other knowledge they had been entrusted with, but were not to share with mankind (Enoch 1(8)1-3).

Evil was already in the world at this point because of Adam's transgression, but now through the sin of the Watchers, evil multiplied upon the face of the earth. The Book of Enoch records God telling the Watchers, *"You have been in heaven, but all the mysteries had not yet been revealed to you, and you knew worthless ones, and these in the hardness of your hearts you have made known to the women, and through these mysteries women and men work much evil on earth"* (Enoch 1(16)3). At this point *"the LORD was sorry that he had made humankind on the earth, and it grieved him to his heart"* (Genesis 6:6, NRSV). So, God decided to destroy all of mankind, except for Noah and his family, who had found favor in the eyes of the Lord. God would make a covenant with Noah and start over with his descendants. And even though these rebellious Watchers would be seized and thrown into the deepest chambers of hell to await the day of judgment, their rebellion would give birth to great evil that continues to plaque mankind till this very day.

The Origin of Demons

When most of Christianity thinks of the forces of evil they usually categorize those forces into two groups, Satan the original rebel in one category, and then every other evil spiritual being is placed into the demon category. Yet, when we read the Scriptures they paint a clear picture of a hierarchy of evil, and even though Satan is at the top of that hierarchy, not all evil spiritual beings should be considered demons. The Apostle Paul helps to clarify this when he writes to the church in Ephesus about the spiritual forces they are struggling against, calling them *rulers, authorities, cosmic powers of this present darkness, and spiritual forces of evil in the heavenly places* (Ephesians 6:12). From this we can see that not every evil rebellious spirit should be classified the same. So, what about the demons the Bible speaks of? How would the first apostles who followed Jesus have understood the idea of demons? An examination of the Second Temple literature can help us to answer these questions and give us a better understanding of the origin of demons and their nature.

Second Temple Jewish literature identifies demons as the disembodied spirits of the giants, who came into being from the union between the Watchers and the daughters of men. The

11

Bible says, "*The Nephilim were on the earth in those days—and also afterward—when the sons of God went in to the daughters of humans, who bore children to them. These were the heroes that were of old, warriors of renown*" (Genesis 6:4, NRSV). Some would try to argue that the Nephilim were not literal giants, but simply famous men or great warriors, yet the Bible makes it clear that they were indeed giants. The children of Israel encounter a remnant of these Nephilim on their way to the promised land. Moses sends out twelve men to spy on the land God had promised to give to them. What these men found caused great fear in all of them, except for Joshua and Caleb. The Scriptures record this, saying, "*So they brought to the Israelites an unfavorable report of the land that they had spied out, saying, 'The land that we have gone through as spies is a land that devours its inhabitants; and all the people that we saw in it are of great size. There we saw the Nephilim (the Anakites come from the Nephilim); and to ourselves we seemed like grasshoppers, and so we seemed to them'*"(Numbers 13:32-33, NRSV).

Josephus, the first century Jewish historian, speaks of the wickedness of the offspring that was produced from the daughters of men and the sons of God, and how they served to multiply wickedness within mankind, saying, "*But for what degree of zeal they had formerly shown for virtue, they now showed by their actions a double degree of wickedness; whereby they made God to be their enemy, for many angels of God accompanied with women, and begat sons that proved unjust, and despisers of all that was good, on account of the confidence they had in their own strength; for the tradition is, That these men did what resembled the acts of those whom the Grecians call giants*" (Antiquities 1(3)72-73). These giants, and their fathers, brought great wickedness upon the earth. And perhaps the Watchers (sons of God) thought their children (the giants/Nephilim) would live long prosperous lives, perhaps they even though they would find some form of immortality amongst mankind, but God had other plans.

Jewish literature, including the Book of Enoch, the Book of Giants, and the Book of Jubilees testify to what became of the race of giants once they died; they became evil spirts, the demonic forces that plaque mankind. The Book of Enoch says of them, *"And now, the giants, who are produced from the spirits and flesh, will be called evil spirits upon the earth, and on the earth will be their dwelling. Evil spirits have proceeded from their bodies; because they are born from men and from the holy Watchers is their beginning and primal origin; they will be evil spirits on earth, and evil spirits will they be called. [As for the spirits of heaven, in heaven will be their dwelling, but as for the spirits of the earth which were born upon the earth, on the earth will be their dwelling.] And the spirits of the giants afflict, oppress, destroy, attack, do battle, and work destruction on the earth, and cause trouble: they take no food, but nevertheless hunger and thirst, and cause offences. And these spirits will rise up against the children of men and against the women, because they have proceeded from them"* (Enoch 1(15)8-12). This is exactly how the first Jewish followers of Jesus, including the Apostles Peter, John, and Paul, would have understood the origin of demons. Other early church fathers understood the origin of demons in the same way, such as Justin Martyr, who wrote, *"But the angels transgressed this appointment, and were captivated by love of women, and begat children who are those that are called demons; and besides, they afterwards subdued the human race to themselves, partly by magical writings, and partly by fears and the punishments they occasioned, and partly by teaching them to offer sacrifices, and incense, and libations, of which things they stood in need after they were enslaved by lustful passions; and among men they sowed murders, wars, adulteries, intemperate deeds, and all wickedness.*"[1]

The demons that plague us today and the demons that Jesus and His first followers encountered during His earthly ministry would seem not to be fallen angels (although they are just as real and active), but rather the disembodied spirits of the giants.

The Council's Rebellion

"God has taken his place in the divine council; in the midst of the gods he holds judgment: 'How long will you judge unjustly and show partiality to the wicked?'" Psalms 82:1-2 (NRSV)

The first rebellion involved Satan and the angels who followed him, the second rebellion involved the Watchers who had sexual affairs with the daughters of men, and the third rebellion we're going to look at involved the divine council of God. Psalms 82 paints a striking picture when it says, *"God has taken his place in the divine council; in the midst of the gods he holds judgment."* Here we have pictured God with His divine council in a court room setting. God is holding judgement against the gods who have ruled unjustly. Now, the question must be asked, what gods is this passage referring to? And where did these gods come from? The answer to both of these questions can be found in verses 6-8 of Psalms 82 when it says, I say, *"You are gods, children of the Most High, all of*

---

[1] Martyr, Justin. "Chapter V: How The Angels Transgressed" in "The Second Apology of Justin for the Christian."

14

you; nevertheless, you shall die like mortals, and fall like any prince. Rise up, O God, judge the earth; or all the nations belong to you!" These gods that the Scriptures speak of here are sons of God, similar to those we looked at from Genesis six, that means they are created spiritual beings, and it would also appear from this passage that these sons of God were placed over the nations to rule on His behalf, but failed to rule justly, even taking glory for themselves.

This can be a hard pill for many Christians to swallow, yet there it is as plain as can be. To better understand this verse we need to examine the Hebrew word *Elohim*. *Elohim* is the word used to depict God in this passage, but it is also used for the word gods. *Elohim* can be used in a singular form or plural; it is used in its singular form to depict the God Most High, and it is also used in its plural form to depict lesser gods who were created by the God Most High. Most High is an important phrase, for it assures us there is no other god like *Yahweh*, another Hebrew phrase that rightly depicts the Most High alone.

Too often the word *Elohim* is wrongly used by many as a name for God, but the Hebrew phrase does not describe the unique qualities of *Yahweh*. Rather, *Elohim* speaks more of where *Yahweh*, the Most High God, resides or the natural state He exists in. When Jesus speaks of God to the Samaritan woman at the well, He says, "*God is spirit*" (John 4:24, NRSV). God's presence certainly fills all of creation, yet at the same time He is spirit and exists in the spiritual realm. So we find that throughout the Scriptures other spiritual beings are also referred to as *Elohim*, such as the gods of the nations, angelic beings, and even the disembodied dead, and although there are other *Elohim* there is no *Elohim* like *Yahweh*. This is why

Moses says, *"Who is like you, O LORD, among the gods? Who is like you, majestic in holiness, awesome in splendor, doing wonders"* (Exodus 15:11, NRSV)? Here Moses refers to the Lord as *Yahweh*, making a clear distinction between Him and the gods of the nation, whom he refers to using an ancient Canaanite phrase for god, *'êl*. In the Old Testament the phrase *'êl* is used to refer to both *Yahweh* and the gods of the nation. When Abram meets Melchizedek, whom the Scripture refer to as the King of Salem and a priest of God Most High, he blesses Abram, saying, *"Blessed be Abram by God Most High, maker of heaven and earth; and blessed be God Most High, who has delivered your enemies into your hand"* (Genesis 14:19-20, NRSV)! The phrase used to describe God Most High here is the Canaanite phrase *'Ēl*, which was also used in the cuneiform clay tablets that were discovered in Ugarit (located in modern day Syria) dating back to around the 13 and 12 century BC to describe the Most High God who created the lesser gods.[2] Melchizedek, who was a priest of the Most High God, living in the land of Canaan would have naturally referred to *Yahweh* as *'Ēl*. *'Ēl* is also the phrase the Scriptures use to describe how *Yahweh* first made himself known to Abraham, Isaac, and Jacob. *"I appeared to Abraham, Isaac, and Jacob as God Almighty, but by my name 'The LORD' I did not make myself known to them"* (Exodus 6:3, NRSV). The phrase for "God Almighty" used here is *'Ēl Šadday*, the phrase for "The Lord" is *Yahweh*. Abraham, who was a part of the Canaanite culture, would have been aware of other gods (sons of God) who were ruling over the nations, but he was also aware that there was no God like *'Ēl Šadday* whom he had given his allegiance to.

---

[2] Cross, Frank Moore. *Canaanite Myth and Hebrew Epic: Essays in the History of the Religion of Israel.* Harvard University Press, 1973

Now that we can see the elohim that are being judged by the Most High Elohim in Psalms 82 are being judged for ruling the nations unjustly, we should answer the question, how did these Elohim come to rule over the nations? The Scriptures say, *"When the Most High apportioned the nations, when he divided humankind, he fixed the boundaries of the peoples according to the number of the gods"* (Deuteronomy 32:8, NRSV). When did God divide humankind? At the Tower of Babel. It was at Babel (Babylon) that the wickedness of mankind was revived again, as they attempted to reach the heavens apart from God. Josephus, the Jewish historian, elaborates on the wicked conditions that led mankind to attempt such an endeavor, saying, *"Now it was Nimrod who excited them to such an affront and contempt of God. He was the grandson of Ham, the son of Noah,--a bold man, and of great strength of hand. He persuaded them not to ascribe it to God as if it was through his means they were happy, but to believe that it was their own courage which procured that happiness. He also gradually changed the government into tyranny,--seeing no other way of turning men from the fear of God, but to bring them into a constant dependence upon his power. He also said he would be revenged on God, if he should have a mind to drown the world again; for that he would build a tower too high for the waters to be able to reach! and that he would avenge himself on God for destroying their forefathers"* (Antiquities 1(4)113-114)! Under the leadership of Nimrod, mankind had rebelled against God, and it would seem to be at this point that God gave control of the nations over to His heavenly council, as He divided the nations.

A quick note to those who may find an objection to Deuteronomy 32:8 because it does not appear the same in all translations. The Masoretic Text, which was used as a translation source for some versions of the Old Testament, such as the King James Version and the New International Version, dates back to around the eleventh century. Which was the oldest version of the Old testament available when the King James Bible was translated. But with the discovery of the Dead Sea Scrolls, which date back to the third and second century BC, and the Septuagint, a Greek translation of the Old Testament, which dates back to the fourth century AD, we have a more ancient source than the Masoretic Text to guide our understanding. And both the Dead Sea Scrolls and the Septuagint agree with each other concerning the Deuteronomy 32:8, as do the writings of the early church fathers.

The sons of God, that is God's heavenly council, were to rule the nations righteously, never taking glory for themselves, but at some point it would seem they were overcome by pride and began to rule in a way that brought glory to themselves instead of their Creator. We find evidence of this in Abraham's saga. First, when Abraham (at the time he was still called Abram, for God had not yet changed his name) goes to Egypt during a time of famine to find relief, he lies about Sarah (at the time Sari) being his wife, for she was beautiful and he thought the people of the land would kill him and take her for themselves, so he tells them she is his sister (which she was), neglecting to tell them that she was also his wife. Sarah's beauty must have been stunning, for she indeed caught the attention of the Egyptians, who told Pharaoh of her beauty, at which point she was brought into the house of Pharaoh. But God protects Sarah and made sure that Pharoah didn't touch her by afflicting Pharaoh and his house with great plagues. Josephus sheds further light on this, saying, *"And when he inquired of the priests, how he might be freed from these calamities, they told him that this his miserable condition was derived from the wrath of God, upon account of his inclination to abuse the stranger's wife"* (Antiquities 1(8)164). Pharaoh doesn't question who God is, but simply returns Sarah to Abraham, and sends him off with great wealth. Fast-forward nearly five hundred years when Moses approaches Pharaoh and commands him to let God's people go, the Pharaoh of that time replies, *"Who is the LORD, that I should heed him and let Israel go? I do not know the LORD, and I will not let Israel go"* (Exodus 5:2, NRSV). The Pharoah during the time of Moses had no idea who the Lord Most High was, yet the Pharaoh during the time of Abraham dares not question the sovereignty of the Most High. At some point after God appointed His council members to rule the nations they rebelled. During Abraham's life the rulers of the nations still had reverence for the Lord Most High, even if they were not actively serving Him, they understood He was above all the gods of the nations.

Likewise, when Abraham is residing in Gerar, the land of the Philistines, he again tells the story that Sarah is only his sister. This time Abimelech, who was king of the Philistines, takes her into his house. The Lord again comes to the rescue of Abraham and Sarah, speaking to Abimelech in a dream, telling him *"You are about to die because of the woman whom you have taken; for she is a married woman"* (Genesis 20:3, NRSV). Abimelech responds, saying, *"Lord, will you destroy an innocent people? Did he not himself say to me, 'She is my sister'? And she herself said, 'He is my brother.' I did this in the integrity of my heart and the innocence of my hands"* (Genesis 20:4-5). Just like Pharaoh who had taken Sarah into his home previously, Abimelech doesn't question who the Lord is, or His sovereignty over the nations, he simply yields to His word. Abimelech, king of the Philistines, who traditionally worshiped the god Dagon, knows who the Lord is, unlike the Pharaoh in the days of Moses. At some point God's council, who were to rule on His behalf, stopped glorifying God and ruling justly, and began to accept the worship that rightly belonged to Yahweh.

The idea of lesser gods who ruled mankind being created by the Most High God can also be found in the works of Hermes Trismegistus, an Egyptian from the Hellenistic Age. Augustine of Hippo, an early church father and theologian, records Hermes proclaiming this idea in a discourse to an individual named Æsculapius, where Hermes says, *"And, since we have undertaken to discourse concerning the relationship and fellowship between men and the gods, know, O Æsculapius, the power and strength of man. As the Lord and Father, or that which is highest, even God, is the maker of the celestial gods, so man is the maker of the gods who are in the temples, content to swell near to men...thus humanity, always mindful of its nature and origin, preserves in the imitation of divinity; and as the Lord and Father made eternal gods, that they should be like Himself, so humanity fashioned its own gods according to the likeliness of its own countenance."*[3] The Egyptian Hermes believed the most High God had created spiritual beings who ruled in Egypt, and who men made images of. Yet, even though they were aware of the Most High God they chose to honor the created spiritual beings (the sons of God) over the one who had created them. It is for this reason the Apostle Paul declares, *"Yes, they knew God, but they wouldn't worship him as God or even give him thanks. And they began to think up foolish ideas*

[3] Augustine. The City of God - Christian Doctrine. Vol. 2: WM. B. Eerdmans Publishing Company, 1979 (pp. 159-160).

of what God was like. As a result, their minds became dark and confused. Claiming to be wise, they instead became utter fools. And instead of worshiping the glorious, ever-living God, they worshiped idols made to look like mere people and birds and animals and reptiles" (Romans 1:21-23, NLT).

If it seems hard to believe that God would allow His spiritual sons to rule on His behalf, consider the vision of the Prophet Micaiah. During the reign of King Ahab of Israel, Micaiah saw a vision of the Lord in His throne room with His heavenly host. The Scriptures record Micaiah telling Ahab, *"I saw the LORD sitting on his throne, with all the host of heaven standing beside him to the right and to the left of him. And the LORD said, 'Who will entice Ahab, so that he may go up and fall at Ramoth-gilead?' Then one said one thing, and another said another, until a spirit came forward and stood before the LORD, saying, 'I will entice him.' 'How?' the LORD asked him. He replied, 'I will go out and be a lying spirit in the mouth of all his prophets.' Then the LORD said, 'You are to entice him, and you shall succeed; go out and do it'"* (1 Kings 22:19-22). God is supreme and doesn't need anyone to help Him rule creation, but He allows His children, both in the spiritual realm and the physical realm to have a part in ruling His creation, but they are expected to do it in a manner that is pleasing to Him and that brings glory to Him; this is something the sons of God (from Psalms 82) who were entrusted to rule the nations failed to do.

Now that we have examined the rebellions of the past, which have served to bring destruction to mankind, let's take a close look at a modern phenomenon that could pose great problems for mankind and the Church…aliens and UFOs.

Chapter 2

Aliens, UFOs, & The Bible

"As I looked at the living creatures, I saw a wheel on the earth beside the living creatures, one for each of the four of them. As for the appearance of the wheels and their construction: their appearance was like the gleaming of beryl; and the four had the same form, their construction being something like a wheel within a wheel." (Ezekiel 1:15-16, NRSV).

Aliens and UFOs…a topic on the fringe, and often laughed at by many biblical scholars, but it is a topic that can no longer be ignored or played down. Blurred pictures and eyewitness reports from what some might consider as less then credible individuals have been replaced by eyewitness reports from Navy Aviators and video recordings of their sightings. No longer are government officials making light of UFO reports or attempting to cover them up, now many of them are searching for answers. Leslie Kean, in her book entitled *UFOs: General, Pilots, and Government Officials go on the Record*, documents many UFO sightings throughout the years that have been reported by credible pilots, both military and commercial, from around the globe, and she points out the many political leaders who are no longer afraid of asking questions about this phenomenon, which can no longer be denied or called a hoax.[4]

The veil has been removed and the evidence must be examined, but what will that evidence proclaim? Will it proclaim that

---

[4] Kean, Leslie (2010). UFOs: Generals, Pilots, and Government Officials go on the Record. Three Rivers Press.

inhabitants from other planets, whose technology is far superior to our own, have created spacecrafts capable of transporting them through light years of space travel, much like many of the Hollywood movies have enacted. Or will the evidence reveal something else, perhaps something much more sinister and evil? And what does the Bible have to say about aliens and life on other planets? Let us examine the evidence and the Scriptures together, and see where this journey of discovery will lead us. We'll start with the concept of life on other planets.

Life on Other Planets

"He determines the number of the stars; he gives to all of them their names" (Psalms 147:4, NRSV).

Does life exist on other planets? It's highly unlikely, and we'll look at exactly why it's unlikely in a moment. But first, could God have created other planets with different or similar forms of life as He did on Earth? Well…He's God, so He can do whatever He wants. But, if there is life on other planets, does that discredit Christianity? No, not at all, the Bible never claims that earth is the only planet that God created life on. Well, if there is life on other planets, would Jesus have to die to redeem them? No, even if there is life on other planets that doesn't mean it was created in the image of God. Mankind was created in God's image, and Adam the first man, sinned against God, causing a curse to pass to all mankind after him, therefore Jesus came to deliver mankind from the curse. The Scriptures declare, *"Yes, Adam's one sin brings condemnation for everyone, but Christ's one act of righteousness brings a right relationship with God and new life for everyone. Because one person disobeyed God, many became sinners. But because one other person obeyed God, many will be made righteous"* (Romans 5:18-19, NLT). And again the Scriptures say, *"But Christ has rescued us from the curse pronounced by the law. When he was hung on the cross, he took upon himself the curse for our wrongdoing. For it is written in the Scriptures, 'Cursed is everyone who is hung on a tree'"* (Galatians 3:13, NLT). Jesus died for the sin of mankind, and even though there are other life forms on Earth, such as dogs, birds, and fish, Christ only died to redeem the one creation that was made in the image of God, man. So, if there is life on other planets, that doesn't mean it was created in the image of God, nor does it mean that Jesus must die to redeem it. Now, let's look at why the possibility of life on other planets is highly unlikely.

The recipe for life to exist on Earth as we know it is very complex, and as we'll see, would not be possible without an intelligent Creator, intentionally placing all the ingredients together in the exact amount required to sustain complex life. Some scientists have come to refer to the place where Earth is placed in our solar system as the Goldilocks Zone; it's not too cold, it's not too hot, and there just the right amount of water for complex life to exist. If the Earth was just 5% closer to the sun it would be too hot to sustain life, and would closely resemble the surface conditions of Venus. Move the Earth back 20% and it would be too cold to sustain life, making its surface conditions similar to Mars. Also, the liquid iron in the Earth's core generates a protective magnetic field around the Earth as it rotates, which is essential for complex life to exist. If the Earth was smaller its core wouldn't be large enough to generate the field size needed to protect the Earth from solar winds, and they would strip our atmosphere away.[5] These are just a few factors that are required to make life possible on Earth.

The list also includes the type of sun we have in our solar system, the size of our moon and its gravitational effect on the Earth, the Earth's atmospheric makeup, in all, there are at least 20 factors that must be met for complex life to exist. And, all these factors have to be just right, they must come together at one time and place if you are going to have a habitable planet like Earth that is capable of sustaining complex life. The odds that all these factors could just accidentality come together in the perfect symphony that is required to produce complex life are astronomical. In fact, some scientist have calculated the odds that all these factors could come together in the perfect symphony required to produce complex life as they have here on Earth to be 0.000000000000001.[6] These facts declare clearly that Earth had a Creator, who perfectly designed her to sustain complex life; life that the Scriptures declare was made in the image of its Creator. *"Then God said, 'Let us make humankind in our image, according to our likeness; and let them have dominion over the fish of the sea, and over the birds of the air, and over the cattle, and over all the wild animals of the earth, and over every creeping thing that creeps upon the earth '"* (Genesis 1:26, NRSV).

So, if these unidentified flying objects, which are now being called unidentified ariel phenomenon by the government, are not coming from other planets, where are they coming from? Jacques Vallee, the famed French scientist who served with the French National Center for Space Studies researching

[5] Gonzalez, G., and J.W. Richards. *The Privileged Planet: How Our Place in the Cosmos Is Designed for Discovery.* Regnery Publishing, 2004.
[6] ibid

unidentified aerospace phenomena, considered an expert on the UFO phenomena, makes it clear in his book entitled *Messengers of Deception*, that although he believes in UFOs he does not believe they are from another world, but rather evil forces that are present in the world, determined to shape this world to their will.[7] Vallee is not the only authoritative figure in the study of UFOs that believes they are real, but not from a planet far-far away. John Keel, in his book entitled *Trojan Horse*, documents the pattern of appearances demonstrated by UFOs throughout the nation (and yes, they do seem to have a pattern), as well as interviewing multiple individuals who claimed to have encountered extraterrestrial life, and as such comes to the same conclusion as Vallee, these UFO's and supposed aliens are not from another planet.[8] Keel presents strong evidence that these UFOs are actually from other dimensions. Keel and Vallee are definitely onto something, and I believe as we examine the Scripture will gain a clearer understanding of exactly what these UFOs and aliens are.

Heavenly Realms

"For our struggle is not against enemies of blood and flesh, but against the rulers, against the authorities, against the cosmic powers of this present darkness, against the spiritual forces of evil in the heavenly places" (Ephesians 6:12, NRSV).

---

[7] Vallee, J. *Messengers of Deception: UFO Contacts and Cults.* Daily Grail Publishing, 2008.

[8] Keel, J.A. *Operation Trojan Horse.* IllumiNet Press, 1996.

The rulers, the authorities, the cosmic powers, and the spiritual forces of evil represent the spiritual forces of darkness that mankind struggles against, especially the followers of Christ. These forces exist in what Paul terms heavenly places, but what exactly does the phrase mean, and where are these heavenly places located? The Greek phrase for heavenly places is *epouranios*, which is derived from two other Greek words, *epi* and *ouranos*. *Epi* means the superimposition of time, place, or order, which is the action of placing one thing over another. *Ouranos* simply means sky or heavens. As we consider these words we can gain a clearer understanding of what God's creation looks like. It would seem that God has created life in different realms, rather than on different planets. In these other realms (or dimensions) exist spiritual beings, which we often refer to as either angels or demons (the good guys and the bad guys). Paul classifies the bad guys as being rulers, authorities, cosmic powers, and spiritual forces of evil. These creatures, who have rebelled against God, exist in the spiritual realm, a realm that appears to overlay our own. A realm from which it would seem they are able to cross over to ours, or at least makes themselves visible to us, when they want to, or perhaps when certain factors (which would be unknown) allow for them to do so. These UFO's and aliens are not creatures from other planets or galaxies far-far away, but rather spiritual beings who have rebelled against the God of all creation, who exist in a realm that overlays our own. Let's consider now the Scriptural and historical evidence for this.

First, when Jesus took Peter, James, and John up to the mountain and was transfigured, undergoing a metamorphosis that changed His appearance and made His clothes into what the Bible describes as dazzling white. The Bible says, *"Then Elijah and Moses appeared and began talking with Jesus"*

(Mark 9:4, NLT). They didn't descend on a cloud, nor were they transported there by some alien spacecraft, they simply appeared. First Jesus was transformed and then Elijah and Moses appeared, it was like the veil that separates the two realms was pulled back for just a moment to expose heavenly realities that changed the appearance of Jesus and made visible Elijah and Moses, and then was pulled back when they were done speaking.

In encouraging the followers of Christ to finish the course God has given them to run in this life, the Book of Hebrews tells us that *"we are surrounded by so great a cloud of witnesses"* (Hebrews 12:1, NRSV). Some would take this passage of Scriptures to be speaking metaphorically here, but it could just as easily be speaking literally. Peter tells us that when the Day of the Lord comes that *"the heavens will pass away with a loud noise, and the elements will be dissolved with fire, and the earth and everything that is done on it will be disclosed"* (2 Peter 3:10, NRSV). The curtain that separates the heavenly realms from the earthly realm will be removed and everything will be made visible. The Book of Revelation paints a similar picture saying, *"The sky vanished like a scroll rolling itself up, and every mountain and island was removed from its place"* (Revelation 6:14, NRSV). The followers of Christ, along with all of humanity, are surrounded by another realm, a spiritual realm that cannot be seen, filled with those who have passed on before us and those whom God created to be spiritual beings.

Consider after the resurrection how Jesus simply appeared to His followers and then disappeared. When the disciples were all in hiding inside a locked house, Jesus suddenly appeared. He didn't come through the door, He didn't come down the chimney, He wasn't transported in from a distant galaxy…He simply appeared, stepping out of the spiritual realm and into the physical realm of His disciples. Again, we see the same principle displayed when Jesus meets with two of His disciples as they travel on the road to Emmaus. At first they didn't realize who was traveling and speaking to them, but when they sat down to eat and the Lord gives thanks for the bread they were about to eat, their eyes were opened and they recognized Him, but as soon as they recognized Him, He vanished right before their eyes, slipping from the physical realm to the spiritual realm.

In the Old Testament, we read about chariots of fire driven by angelic charioteers. The Prophet Elijah and Elisha were separated by such a chariot before a whirlwind took him to the heavenly realms. The Bible records this event saying, "*As they were walking along and talking, suddenly a chariot of fire appeared, drawn by horses of fire. It drove between the two men, separating them, and Elijah was carried by a whirlwind into heaven*" (2 Kings 2:11, NLT). Likewise, after Elijah is gone and Elisha is serving in his place as a prophet in Israel, there comes a moment when the king of Aram seeks to capture him. The king discovered where Elisha was staying, he sent a great army to capture him. When Elisha's servant saw the great army he was terrified, but Elisha assured him there was no need to worry, saying, "*Do not be afraid, for there are more with us than there are with them. Then Elisha prayed: O LORD, please open his eyes that he may see. So the LORD opened the eyes of the servant, and he saw; the mountain was full of horses and chariots of fire all around Elisha*" (2 Kings 6:16-17, NRSV). Elisha had an army of spiritual warriors sent by God to protect him, an army only he could see. Even though no one else could see the army, until he asked God to open the eyes of his servant, it didn't diminish the truth that the prophet was protected by the forces of heaven that existed in the spiritual realm, but were able to fight and defend Elisha in the physical realm if need be. The Book of Psalms reminds us of the angelic protection the children of God have, saying, *"For he will order his angels to protect you wherever you go. They will hold you up with their hands so you won't even hurt your foot on a stone"* (Psalms 91:11-12, NLT).

Not only do we find such spiritual reference recorded in Scriptural history, but we also find it in the secular history record. Before the Jewish revolt that led to the destruction of the Temple in 70AD, Josephus records the manifestation of spiritual warriors over the skies of Jerusalem, saying, *"A certain extraordinary and incredible phenomenon appeared; I suppose the account of it would seem to be a fable, were it not related by those that saw it, and were not the events that followed it of so considerable a nature as to deserve such signals; for, before sunsetting, chariots and troops of soldiers in their armor were seen running about among the clouds, and surrounding of cities"* (Antiquities 6 (5) 297-299). Likewise, Tacitus the ancient Roman historian, records similar events that took place in Jerusalem before the destruction of the Temple, saying, *"There had been seen hosts joining battle in the skies, the fiery gleam of arms, the temple illuminated by a sudden radiance from the clouds. The doors of the inner shrine were suddenly thrown open, and a voice of more than mortal tone was heard to cry that the Gods were departing"* (Histories 5.13). How easy would it be for an ancient astronaut theorist who is steeped in the Hollywood culture of space aliens, instead of the Scriptures and history, to conclude such spiritual manifestations were UFOs.

Culture has a profound effect on the way we understand the world around us. It defines the norms and values of a people group, how they perceive, categorize, and makes sense of the world they live in. Our cultural understanding of the spiritual realm has been defined by the movie industry. From the 1930s TV series *Flash Gordon* that captured the imagination of kids and adults alike, to Steven Spielberg's *Close Encounters of the Third Kind* and George Lucas' *Star Wars*, which continues in popularity today, American cinema has shaped the way most people (including the followers of Christ) perceive the supernatural. Instead of understanding UFO sightings through the lens of Scripture and history, they interpret them in accordance with a worldview that has been shaped by American cinema. Thus ancient astronaut theorists look at verses from Ezekiel and Isaiah and believe these prophets recorded images of flying saucers and aliens, failing to understand that these visions the prophets recorded, although representative of heavenly realities that affected the world the prophets lived in, were not literal imagery of objects or beings that existed in heaven. These images were meant to relay heavenly truths to the prophets and those they wrote to. For example, when John sees an image of a woman sitting on a scarlet beast that was full of blasphemous names, having seven heads and ten horns (Revelation chapter 17), it was not an image that was to be taken literal, as if there was a terrifying dragon out there with many heads that an evil queen was riding upon seeking to bring destruction on mankind. No, not at all, but that is the understanding a worldview shaped by American cinema would give you. Fortunately for John and us, the angel with him interprets the image for him, so that we're not left wondering what it means, or allowing Hollywood to interpret it for us. The same holds true for the images Ezekiel and Isaiah

31

see in their heavenly visions, they are not literal images, but rather they are representative of heavenly truths that directly affect our earthly realities. But, if we do not hold a biblical worldview we will find ourselves understanding these visions, and the images of unidentified object in the skies, from an American cinematic worldview. The objects in our skies that have been observed by naval pilots and others around the world, should be taken seriously, but we cannot interpret those objects from a worldview that has been shaped by Hollywood, we must interpret them from a biblical worldview that is supported by historical fact.

Alien Contact

"False messiahs and false prophets will appear and produce signs and omens, to lead astray, if possible, the elect. But be alert; I have already told you everything" (Mark 13:22-23, NRSV)

Satan and his forces of darkness will use any method they find effective to draw people from Christ and to keep them from experiencing the fullness of life God has prepared for them; UFOs and aliens who contact people are just two of their newest methods. Once, these evil spiritual forces posed as gods who had come down to help and bless mankind, now people are familiar with science and science fiction, so they pass themselves off as aliens from a distant galaxy who have come to help the human race to advance. When reading reports of those who have been contacted by aliens it is easy to find commonalities that draw all their stories together. First, the aliens assure them that they have come to help mankind, and have chosen them to be their representative. They promise them they have great secrets to pass on to the people of earth that will make the world a better place. Second, they challenge the way mankind is currently living; their social, political, and religious systems. Thirdly, they often attack Christianity in some way. In many cases they claim Jesus was an alien, or that they have additional truths to add to the Bible. Jacques Vallee and John Keel have both done a great job interviewing those who claim to have been contacted by aliens, and have found many of them to be sincere in their beliefs, but the same commonalities are woven throughout all of their reports: a belief that they have been chosen by the aliens to help usher in a new-age for mankind, where the political, social and religious systems (especially Christianity) of the world will be revamped to make the world a better place.

One of the most famous alien contact stories is that of George Adamski in 1952. Adamski claimed to have been contacted by beings from Venus, who spoke to him through hand gestures and some form of mental telepathy. His story was published in the widely popular work entitled *Flying Saucers Have Landed*. Adamski maintained these alien visitors were nervous about mankind's current path, fearful that their pursuit of nuclear weapons could not only bring destruction on humanity, but could also have devastating effects for beings on other planets. Adamski also said the Venusians believed in God but they communicated to him that the people of Earth had a shallow understanding of the Creator, and that there was a much broader picture of who God was and how He worked, a picture that the people of Earth did not understand.

Recently I've witnessed an individual on *Facebook* be seduced by such evil spiritual forces, claiming he had been contacted by aliens, and now he was doing all he could to lead others to believe in them. In his efforts to convince people to embrace these creatures, he concludes that God is working through them, and when asked what makes him think that God is involved, he responded:

It's a personal relationship I developed with them in 2019. It's a long story but they asked me to allow them to fix my ailing back and I agreed to it under certain terms… it didn't effect anything w/ me getting to Heaven, I would never deny Jesus as my Lord and savior, I would need help getting family and friends to understand all this and last I would be back before my wife woke up lol… Well that night something amazing happened, they fixed a hurt back that I couldn't even put my socks and shoes on without tears running down my face it hurt so bad. They repaired it that night and it's never hurt again since. My part of the deal was that they asked for help explaining to Humans when they show up to all that they come in PEACE LOVE and UNITY, they are made from the same God we are made from, they respect all of our religions that represent PEACE LOVE and UNITY. They have the technology needed to clean the pollution from Earth much faster and cleaner than we do. They can take a mountain of our pollution and turn it into a minimal amount then send it to be burned at the sun…. They solar charge and Lunar charge daily, they even use streetlights to charge.. They have already been cleaning our air and water from the vapor plasma clouds right above our heads for a while now.. They communicate w/ me on a regular basis.. It's the most peace I've ever felt by when I'm out recording or hanging out with them… There's not a lot more to my story but all in all…How do I know? They told me.

When dealing with the spiritual forces of evil that disguise themselves as alien saviors who have come to deliver mankind, the followers of Christ would do well to heed the words of the Apostle Paul who said, *"Even Satan disguises himself as an angel of light. So it is no wonder that his servants also disguise themselves as servants of righteousness. In the end they will get the punishment their wicked deeds deserve"* (2 Corinthians 11:14-15, NLT). As the accounts given by supposed alien contactees are closely examined, it becomes clear that there is a direct connection to Satan and the occult.

Aliens and the Occult

"There shall not be found among you anyone who makes his son or his daughter pass through the fire, or one who practices witchcraft, or a soothsayer, or one who interprets omens, or a sorcerer, or one who conjures spells, or a medium, or a spiritist, or one who calls up the dead"
(Deuteronomy 18:10-11, NKJ).

As we consider the connection between aliens and the occult, we must give attention to how a connection is often made between the supposed aliens and the individuals they are making contact with. Contact is often reported to be made not in a face-to-face encounter but rather through some other form of occultism communication style such as, séances, Ouija boards, or some form of transcendental meditation.

Another contactee story that helps to clearly identify the connection between the occult and alien encounters is that of George Van Tassel. In the 1950s Van Tassel claimed to have been contacted by alien entities through channeled transmission (similar to telepathy), rather than face-to-face contact. Chief among these entities was Ashtar. According to Van Tassel, Ashtar was the commander of a fleet of spacecrafts that surrounded the Earth. Although Van Tassel was the first to report making contact with Ashtar, he would not be the last, many others have subsequently claimed to have made contact with him through means of channeled transmissions. Yet, this is not the first time we find Ashtar mentioned in the history of mankind. The name Ashtar first appears in ancient Near Eastern text dating back to around 1200BC that were found in the old city of Ugarit.

Ashtar is spoken of in the Ugaritic text as being one of the Canaanite gods that were worshipped. He was known as the Day Star who sought to sit on the throne of Baal (also called El), who was the most high god in the Canaanite pantheon of gods, but was unable to and thus was cast down.[9] The Ugaritic text records this, saying:

> *Let Ashtar the Tyrant be king."-*
> *Straightway Ashtar the Tyrant*
> > *Goes up to the Fastness of Zaphon*
> > *(And) sits on Baal Puissant's throne.*
> *(But) his feet reach not down to the footstool,*
> > *Nor his head reaches up to the top.*
> *So Ashtar the Tyrant declares:*
> > *"I'll not reign in Zaphon's Fastness!"*
> *Down goes Ashtar the Tyrant,*
> > *Down from the throne of Baal Puissant,*
> > *And reigns in El's Earth, all of it.*[10]

---

[9] Collins, John (1992). The Book of Daniel (pp. 29-35). In The Anchor Bible Dictionary (Vol. 2). Doubleday Publishing.

[10] Pritchard, James (1958). The Ancient Near East: An Anthology of Texts and Pictures. Princeton Press. (p. 112).

The story should sound familiar, for it very much parallels Isaiah's account of the expulsion of Satan from Heaven, which we looked at in chapter one.

> *"How you are fallen from heaven, O Day Star, son of Dawn! How you are cut down to the ground, you who laid the nations low! You said in your heart, 'I will ascend to heaven; I will raise my throne above the stars of God; I will sit on the mount of assembly on the heights of Zaphon; I will ascend to the tops of the clouds, I will make myself like the Most High.' But you are brought down to Sheol, to the depths of the Pit"* (Isaiah 14:12-15, NRSV).

Comparing the Scriptures to the Ugaritic text, and the accounts of individuals who claimed to have made contact with the alien entity known as Ashtar, we can make a clear connection between the occult and aliens. We can also make the conclusion that this Ashtar is not an alien entity from a distant galaxy, who commands a fleet of spaceships that surround the Earth, but rather he is whom Paul referred to as the god of this world, Satan, commanding a host of demonic spiritual beings aimed at bringing destruction to mankind through deceit and treachery, as they assume the role of space aliens from a distant galaxy. Paul tells the church in Corinth, *"Satan, who is the god of this world, has blinded the minds of those who don't believe. They are unable to see the glorious light of the Good News. They don't understand this message about the glory of Christ, who is the exact likeness of God"* (2 Corinthians 4:4, NLT).

Satan and his forces of darkness do all they can to bring destruction and ruin to the lives of those God loves, which is all of humanity. They will use any means necessary to accomplish their sinister mission, and posing as aliens from a distant galaxy is simply their newest method, and it's proving to be successful, for too many have had their understanding of this world shaped by the movie industry, rather than relying on the Word of God to guide them in their view of the world.

Refuse to buy into the deceitful lies of the enemy! See these alien forces for what they truly are; they are evil rulers and authorities of the unseen world, mighty powers in this dark world, and evil spirits in the heavenly places seeking to work out their sinister plan of destruction on mankind, and not alien saviors from a distant galaxy. Don't believe the liar, and the liar will have no power over your life!

A Trojan Horse

"These people are false apostles. They are deceitful workers who disguise themselves as apostles of Christ. But I am not surprised! Even Satan disguises himself as an angel of light. So it is no wonder that his servants also disguise themselves as servants of righteousness. In the end they will get the punishment their wicked deeds deserve" (2 Corinthians 11:13-15, NLT).

In Greek mythology the Trojan Horse was a large wooden horse used during the Trojan War by the Greeks to deceive the people of Troy. The Greeks hid a small contingent of soldiers in the horse and pretended to sail off after a ten-year siege. The people of Troy thought they had won the victory, and unwittingly brought the wooden horse into the city as a trophy to celebrate their triumph over the mighty Greeks. But, that night when everyone went to sleep, the small contingent of troops that were hiding in the horse snuck out, opened the city gates, letting the Greeks in, who destroyed the seemingly invincible city of Troy. The Greeks effectively used deception as a powerful weapon to accomplish something that years of direct conflict could not do.

I believe the current UFO sightings and alien contact tales are nothing more than a Trojan Horse. A cleverly devised plan by Satan and the forces of darkness that he commands to bring destruction to humanity, using deception and cunning. During the Watcher Rebellion that's recorded in Genesis chapter six, the Book of Enoch tells us that the Watchers taught mankind forbidden knowledge. They gave mankind the knowledge to read the stars and the signs of the Earth and moon, to work with the metals of the Earth to make weapons of war so that they could destroy one another. These Watchers may have seemed like emissaries from the heavens freely giving mankind the knowledge they needed to advance and achieve new heights, but all they truly did was multiply sin and death on the earth. They were not emissaries from the heavens with good intentions, bringing God's will to man, but rather they were heavenly rebels leading mankind away from the one true God; they were emissaries of death.

Beware the Trojan Horse the adversary has set up! These UFOs and aliens are not appearing to us as messengers of hope and revival, they are messengers of death, just like the Watchers who first rebelled against God. Their future is the Lake of Fire that was prepared for the Devil and his angels, and they would love nothing more than to take mankind with them. Why would they do such a thing? Perhaps it's because God loves mankind and sent His Son to rescue them from the clutches of Death and the Grave, and they seek to bring hurt to God in this way, or perhaps it's just because of their evil nature. Whatever their reasons, we must recognize these UFO sightings and alien contacts for what they are, deceptive works of Satan and his dark kingdom. Always remember, if you believe a liar you empower the liar. Jesus said Satan is the father of lies, and if you buy into Satan's deception about UFOs and aliens, you'll give him the ability, and the opportunity, to bring destruction to your life. UFOs and aliens are nothing more than a carefully constructed Trojan Horse, fashioned by Satan and his forces of darkness, who exist in the heavenly realms, to bring death and ruin to mankind.

Now that we better understand the spiritual forces that have rebelled against God and seek to lead mankind astray, bringing destruction and ruin to their lives, we can begin to examine our role in this struggle. Jesus has surely won the victory on the cross, and the spiritual forces of evil have been judged guilty and will one day receive their eternal punishment, but until that day comes the war for the souls of mankind will rage on. You have a vital part in that war!

Chapter 3

The War

"For we are not fighting against flesh-and-blood enemies, but against evil rulers and authorities of the unseen world, against mighty powers in this dark world, and against evil spirits in the heavenly places." Ephesians 6:12 (NLT)

C.S. Lewis, in his work entitled The Screwtape Letters, documents a fictional correspondence between two demons. The two demons are represented as an uncle and a nephew. They are involved in a mentor - mentee relationship in which Screwtape tries to direct his nephew Wormwood in causing destruction in the life of the man he has been assigned to. In the second letter, it is revealed that the man Wormwood has been assigned to has been saved, but Screwtape relieves Wormwood in his present failure with these words:

> *"One of our great allies at present is the Church itself. Do not misunderstand me. I do not mean the Church as we see her spread out through all time and space and rooted in eternity, terrible as an army with banners. That, I confess, is a spectacle which makes our boldest tempters uneasy. But fortunately it is quite invisible to these humans. All your patient sees is the half-finished, sham Gothic erection on the new building estate."*

Screwtape comforts Wormwood in his belief that even though the man is saved, and is now going to church, that he will never realize what the true Church is, or the power it carries in the battle against the forces of darkness it is to be engaged in.

Although this is a fictional tale, like many of C.S. Lewis' fictional writings, it reveals tremendous Scriptural truths!

The Church of Jesus Christ is much greater than any single building or denomination, and the war the Church (made up of all believers in Christ) is to be involved in, against the satanic forces of darkness has for the most part gone ignored by too many believers! Unfortunately for the body of Christ the enemy has been relatively successful in deceiving much of today's Church!

> *"The first step on the way to victory is to recognize the enemy." ~ Corrie Ten Boom*

Our enemy is real, and so is the war we are engaged in!

In Revelation 12, John records a series of visions that tell of Satan's rebellion against God, his expulsion from heaven, and his efforts to destroy the Church of Jesus Christ; a Church that is spread out through time and space, rooted in eternity, powerful and mighty. John writes of the enemy's struggle against the Church saying, "*So when the dragon saw that he had been thrown down to the earth, he pursued the woman who had given birth to the male child. But the woman was given the two wings of the great eagle, so that she could fly from the serpent into the wilderness, to her place where she is nourished for a time, and times, and half a time. Then from his mouth the serpent poured water like a river after the woman, to sweep her away with the flood. But the earth came to the help of the woman; it opened its mouth and swallowed the river that the dragon had poured from his mouth. Then the dragon was angry with the woman, and went off to make war on the rest of her children, those who keep the commandments of God and hold the testimony of Jesus*" (Revelation 12:13-17, NRSV). The woman in John's vision represents the Church eternal, spread throughout time and space, and her children represent the individuals of mankind who have placed their trust in Jesus Christ as Lord and Savior, they hold the testimony of Jesus and they are the children of the Most High. The serpent and dragon imagery are representations of Satan and his dark kingdom, they can do nothing to hurt the Church eternal, for she is under the covering protection of Heaven. Therefore, Satan and his dark kingdom go forth to oppose the children of God, making war against them and the world they live in, looking to bring destruction and ruin to all they touch.

God's children must have a firm understanding that their struggle is never against flesh and blood, but rather the evil spiritual forces that lead and direct the flesh and blood that are working to destroy and abolish the work of Christ!

The enemy realizes that if he can misdirect our efforts and energies into fighting against flesh and blood, ignoring the spiritual realities that operate in the heavenlies, which are actually directing the human efforts that oppose the children of God, he can win the battle; for he knows the final war has already been won!

In this war you are to be engaged in, you will find the struggle reaching out to three major areas. A struggle for the lost souls of mankind, for the potential God has placed within you, and for world order. We'll take a closer look at each of these now.

Describe the spiritual war the Church is involved in?

_____

_____

How do you see your role in this war?

_____

_____

_____

_____

How does this spiritual war affect the physical realm?

_____

_____

_____

_____

Every war produces casualties. What kind of casualties does this war against the evil forces of darkness produce?

_____

_____

_____

_____

For Mankind

"If the Good News we preach is hidden behind a veil, it is hidden only from people who are perishing. Satan, who is the god of this world, has blinded the minds of those who don't believe. They are unable to see the glorious light of the Good News. They don't understand this message about the glory of Christ, who is the exact likeness of God." 2 Corinthians 4:3-4 (NLT)

The battle for the souls of mankind is real! And it carries eternal consequences!

Jesus has won the war over sin and death through His crucifixion and resurrection, but Satan still seeks to blind the eyes of men and women to the salvation which is found through Jesus Christ! So, we the Church of Jesus Christ are engaged in warfare, battling for the souls of mankind throughout the Earth!

Jesus has done His part on the cross, and committed the rest to His Church! The souls of mankind have, in a sense, been entrusted to the Church of Jesus Christ. There is no question who will win the war between God and Satan for planet Earth. It has already been decided, but the fight for the lost souls on planet Earth is an ongoing struggle.

The enemy seeks to keep mankind blinded. Our responsibility is to meet the devil on the battlefield of prayer, defeating him there by the Word of God and the power of the Holy Spirit. Then we, the army of The Lord, must go to the lost of this world with the life-saving message of the Gospel of Jesus Christ! *"For I am not ashamed of the gospel of Christ, for it is*

the power of God to salvation for everyone who believes..."
(Romans 1:16, NKJ).

> *"But have we Holy Spirit power - power that restricts the devil's power, pulls down strongholds and obtains promises? Daring delinquents will be damned if they are not delivered from the devil's dominion. What has hell to fear other than a God-anointed, prayer-powered church?"* ~ Leonard Ravenhill

The Church must recognize the struggle they are to be involved in! Then we must engage the enemy with all the might of the Holy Spirit and the Word of God!

The enemy shows little concerns over the church that would serve as a social club or an adult baby-sitting service! But the church that would embrace their responsibility of rescuing the lost from the fires of Hell will find the war against the enemy ever so real, for the forces of darkness will not lie down and allow us to claim the souls of the lost without a fight!

It is only by the name of Jesus that men and women around the world may be saved! For this reason, the adversary will do all he can to propagate false religions, and to corrupt the simple and eternal truth of the Gospel message!

> *"By a Carpenter mankind was made, and only by that can mankind be remade."* ~ Desiderius Erasmus

The enemy does all he can to blind the eyes of the lost to the simple truth of the Gospel message, and to keep the Church of Jesus Christ idle and out of the affairs of their Father!

Time is short and the task is great! We must be ever aware of the war we are in, and the prize of the souls of mankind we are to fight for, and win, for our King, Jesus Christ!

The followers of Christ must understand their role as soldiers, enlisted in the Lord's army, refusing to get sidetracked by the cares of this world and the desires of the flesh! *"Join with me in suffering, like a good soldier of Christ Jesus. No one serving as a soldier gets entangled in civilian affairs, but rather tries to please his commanding officer"* (2 Timothy 2:3-4, NIV).

As we set out to fight the enemy for the souls of mankind how can we resist the enemy in his attempts to blind the lost to the saving grace which is found in no other but Jesus?

_____

_____

_____

_____

Talk about the devil's strategy to keep the Church blind to the war that they are to be engaged in?

_____

_____

_____

_____

Name at least two things you can do to make sure you stay engaged in the struggle for the souls of mankind.

_____

_____

_____

_____

For Your Kingdom Potential

"For we are God's masterpiece. He has created us anew in Christ Jesus, so we can do the good things he planned for us long ago." Ephesians 2:10 (NLT)

God has masterfully crafted each of His children to expand His Kingdom in a very special and unique manner, while at the same time working in harmony with the rest of His children!

When we call on Jesus for salvation, God creates us anew in Christ, so that we may fulfill the grand plan He has created for our lives! To be certain, that plan will be starkly different than the plans we have crafted for ourselves. God's plan is sure to be filled with good works that will bring glory to Jesus Christ, destroying the works of the devil, and expanding the Kingdom; all at the same time!

God told the prophet Jeremiah, *"I knew you before I formed you in your mother's womb. Before you were born I set you apart and appointed you as my prophet to the nations"* (Jeremiah 1:5, NLT). Before Jeremiah was ever born, God had crafted an incredible plan for his life, and when Jeremiah reached a point where he surrendered his life to God's will that plan went into action, and Jeremiah became a powerful force for the Kingdom of his God. The same is true for you, before you were born God crafted a magnificent plan for your life, and when you called out to Jesus for salvation that plan went into effect. Continue to surrender your will to the Lord, so that you may achieve all He has called you to. Always keep in mind the words the Lord spoke to the children of Israel, for they have implications for your life today as well. *"For I know the plans I have for you, says the LORD. They are plans for good and not for disaster, to give you a future and a hope"* (Jeremiah 29:11, NLT). God has a grand future prepared for you, a future that the adversary wants to steal; stay submitted to the Lord and you will surely experience the future and hope He has prepared for you!

Still, with this certainty in hand, we find too many of God's children are trapped in the cycle of accidentally living for the Kingdom of God. They have been blinded to the truth and deceived by the enemy into believing their lives are meant for another purpose other than that which God has prepared for them.

The enemy knows he cannot steal our salvation, so the next best thing he can do, and he does it very well, is to steal our Kingdom potential!

We must embrace the fact that we have been given an eternal purpose with our rebirth in Christ Jesus! And, that eternal purpose will never be fulfilled if we allow the enemy to deceive us, causing us to focus on our own desire and not those of Christ.

An eternal purpose requires eternal effort to be fulfilled, and when this is done it yields an eternal reward!

As a child of the Most High God you must step out in the full power of the Holy Spirit, striving with all the Spirit's might to fulfill that which God has prepared for you to achieve for His glorious Kingdom! Being an average pew-sitting Christian cannot be an option for you. You are called to a much grander destiny as a representative of Christ Jesus in this life!

> *"Refuse to be average. Let your heart soar as high as it will." ~ A.W. Tozer*

The devil tried to steal the potential of Jesus by using Peter; Christ understood the problem wasn't Peter, but the enemy who was directing Peter's words and actions. *"Jesus turned and said to Peter, 'Get behind me, Satan! You are a stumbling block to me; you do not have in mind the concerns of God, but merely human concerns'"* (Matthew 16:23, NIV).

Understanding where the true battle lied, Jesus was able to successfully confront, and overcome, the forces of evil that attempted to steal His God given potential. Jesus knew His struggle was not against flesh and blood. He successfully directed His energy and efforts towards the spiritual realities that were controlling His present physical realities.

The enemy will use every advantage he can to steal your God given potential! He will tempt you with the things you desire, he will use your friends and loved ones to pull you off course, he will attempt to afflict your physical body, and even the bodies of your children and loved ones to keep you from fulfilling the purpose for which you were created anew.

If you understand who is trying to destroy you, and steal your Kingdom potential, you can confront the enemy and defeat him as Jesus did!

"No individual has any right to come into the world and go out of it without leaving something behind." ~ *George Washington Carver*

You are called to eternally IMPACT the world for Jesus Christ! You have been given the power of the Holy Spirit and the eternal Word of God to ensure your success! Your life is to be a life of significance, eternal significance, which continues to IMPACT the world long after you have left it!

In what way is your life making an eternal difference for the Kingdom of God?

_____

_____

_____

_____

In general, we have all been called to fulfill the Great Commission, but what uniquely, within that general calling, has God created you anew to do?

_____

_____

_____

_____

How has the enemy tried to keep you from fulfilling your Kingdom potential? And has he been successful?

_____

_____

_____

_____

What are at least three steps you can take to ensure you fulfill your God given destiny, preventing the enemy from stealing your Kingdom potential here in this life?

_____

_____

_____

_____

For World Order

"Don't love the world's ways. Don't love the world's goods. Love of the world squeezes out love for the Father. Practically everything that goes on in the world—wanting your own way, wanting everything for yourself, wanting to appear important—has nothing to do with the Father. It just isolates you from him." 1 John 2:15-16 (MSG)

When God created Adam and Eve, He gave them the task of setting up a governing system on planet earth that fell in line with His standard of doing things. *"And God blessed them [granting them certain authority] and said to them, 'Be fruitful, multiply, and fill the earth, and subjugate it [putting it under your power]; and rule over (dominate) the fish of the sea, the birds of the air, and every living thing that moves upon the earth'"* (Genesis 1:28, AMP).

Adam and Eve bore the responsibility of filling the earth with God's glorious rule; to bring it, and keep it, under the subjugation of heavenly realities. The world system was to emulate the glory of its Creator! But, when Adam sinned, he surrendered the authority God had given him to rule on the earth and set up Kingdom realities to Satan.

> *"And as men's diversions increase from the world, so do their entanglements from Satan. When they have more to do in the world than they can well manage, they shall have more to do from Satan than they can well withstand." ~ John Owen*

At that point, the enemy began setting up a governing system upon planet earth that emulated his evil nature. Greed, pride, sickness, disease, poverty, lust…all of these are part of the devil's world system. It's a system which he has set up around the world to govern under his rule, a system he has sadly used to infiltrate the Church with, holding God's people captive under his illegitimate rule.

> *"How much of these destructive elements, esteemed by men, does the devil bring into the church, until all the high, unworldly and holy aims, and heavenly objects of the church are retired and forgotten?" ~ E.M. Bounds*

When Jesus was resurrected, He told His followers He had been given all authority in Heaven and on earth. The authority

Adam lost, authority he was to use in setting up a world order upon planet earth that fell in line with God's will, has been taken back by Jesus! It was with the announcement of this news that Jesus commissioned His follower to go throughout all the earth making disciples of all mankind.

Today the followers of Jesus Christ are still commissioned to go throughout the world with the authority of their King destroying the realities and the world system the enemy has set up, establishing new Kingdom realities on planet earth that reflect the glory of their Lord!

In place of sickness we bring healing! In place of poverty we bring abundant provision! In place of sin and death we bring the salvation of our Lord! We, as representatives of the Lord bring the will of God, and the realities of Heaven, to the world around us! We are charged with ensuring God's will is done on earth as it is in Heaven!

What does it mean to you to govern the world as a representative of Christ?

_____

_____

_____

_____

How can you successfully do this?

_____

_____

_____

_____

What could hinder you from doing this?

_____

_____

_____

_____

How could this hindrance be overcome?

_____

_____

_____

_____

Chapter 4

The Strongman

"If Satan has risen up against himself and is divided, he cannot stand, but he is finished! But no one can enter the strong man's house and plunder his property unless he first binds the strong man, and then he will plunder his house."
Mark 3:26-27 (NASB)

The strong man's house that Jesus plundered was Satan. Jesus demolished the power of sin and death which the enemy used to hold all of mankind captive. Although this is an absolute truth, Satan and his henchmen are not powerless; they are still active, deceptive, and cunning.

The positional hierarchy of the evil spirit will determine the amount of power he is able to exert on those he attempts to oppress. Consider the father who brought his demon possessed son to the disciples for help, even though the disciples had cast out demons before, this one was much stronger and their immediate efforts proved unfruitful. The Gospel of Mark records the incident saying, *"And when He came to the disciples, He saw a great multitude around them, and scribes disputing with them. Immediately, when they saw Him, all the people were greatly amazed, and running to Him, greeted Him. And He asked the scribes, 'What are you discussing with them?' Then one of the crowd answered and said, 'Teacher, I brought You my son, who has a mute spirit. And wherever it seizes him, it throws him down; he foams at the mouth, gnashes his teeth, and becomes rigid. So I spoke to Your disciples, that they should cast it out, but they could not'"* (Mark 9:14-18, NKJV). The man was understandably troubled, not only was his son possessed by a demon, but he also found no help for his son with the disciples. Jesus cast the demon from the boy, freeing him from the torment of the evil spirit. Later the disciples of Jesus ask Him why they were unable to cast the demon from the boy themselves, for they had performed such miracles in the past. Jesus responds saying, *"This kind can come out by nothing but prayer and fasting"* (Mark 9:29, NKJV). This evil spirit was more powerful than the ones the disciples had encountered in the past, and for them to overcome such a spirit they would need to be strengthened through prayer and fasting. Prayer and fasting are a powerful combination that should not be overlooked when you're facing great challenges and need a real breakthrough!

As we set out to advance the Kingdom we must recognize the work and reality of the enemy, as well as the strength and power he is capable of exerting. Because the enemy is capable of exerting great power we must not hesitate to confront him in the authority and power we have been entrusted with.

In our efforts to expand the Kingdom we will undoubtedly come into contact with different levels of spiritual evil, but before we can destroy their work and establish Kingdom realities, we must first bind them.

> *"The devil is the strong man, the giant robber. He holds men in possession as a warrior holds his property. There is no getting his goods from him without first encountering himself. The bare idea of spoiling him while you are his friend, or he is unsubdued, is ridiculous." ~ Charles Spurgeon*

Through Christ we have the power to bind the enemy and lay waste to his works! *"Listen carefully: I have given you authority [that you now possess] to tread on serpents and scorpions, and [the ability to exercise authority] over all the power of the enemy (Satan); and nothing will [in any way] harm you"* (Luke 10:19, AMP).

As we operate in the name of our Lord Jesus Christ, representing Him and His interest here on planet earth, we carry His authority and the power of the Holy Spirit, to assert ourselves over all the powers, dominions, and works of the enemy!

> *"God's children who have entered into His victory by the Cross, also know something of what it is to bind the strong one. His Cross is the force that sets us free to spoil the house of the strong one, and rescue other souls." ~ G. Campbell Morgan*

We must embrace the victory that has been won for us by Jesus Christ! Jesus has given us a Great Mission, and there can be no doubt that the adversary will do everything in his power to hinder that Mission. But, if we understand the authority and power we have been given, Satan and his dark kingdom don't stand a chance!

How would you describe the *strongman* and his *work*?

_____

_____

_____

_____

How have you confronted the forces of darkness in the past?

_____

_____

_____

_____

Territorially Assigned

"But for twenty-one days the spirit prince of the kingdom of Persia blocked my way. Then Michael, one of the archangels, came to help me, and I left him there with the spirit prince of the kingdom of Persia." Daniel 10:13 (NLT)

Satan is not omnipresent, nor is he omniscient, but he is a master at networking through a vast array of evil spirits, organized in a seemingly military hierarchy, which has been designed to undermine mankind's encounter with the Kingdom of God in every way possible.

Through this diabolical network, the enemy is capable of infiltrating governments, various institutions, educational systems, media, and religious bodies. Working in a unified format through this diabolical networking structure Satan is able to enact his destructive plan for mankind throughout the world.

As we saw in our discussion in chapter one on Psalms 82 and Deuteronomy 32:8, evil rebellious spiritual beings have taken up geographical control over the nations. Originally given this control by God to represent Him, they have rebelled against the Lord and now bring chaos and devastation to the world.

Through this spiritual network the adversary has been able to successfully implement much of his evil- destructive schemes in the lives of mankind.

The writings of Daniel provide further evidence for a militaristic governing system in which evil spirits oversee geographical regions bringing havoc, deception, and death. Consider the words spoken by the Lord's angel to Daniel after his twenty-one days of fasting and mourning. *"Don't be afraid, Daniel. Since the first day you began to pray for understanding and to humble yourself before your God, your request has been heard in heaven. I have come in answer to your prayer. But for twenty-one days the spirit prince of the kingdom of Persia blocked my way. Then Michael, one of the archangels, came to help me, and I left him there with the spirit prince of the kingdom of Persia"* (Daniel 10:12-13, NLT). He further tells him, *"Do you know why I have come? Soon I must return to fight against the spirit prince of the kingdom of Persia, and after that the spirit prince of the kingdom of Greece will come. Meanwhile, I will tell you what is written in the Book of Truth. (No one helps me against these spirit princes except Michael, your spirit prince"* (Daniel 10:20-21, NLT). The words of the Lord's angel paints an incredible picture of Satan's dark kingdom and how it is spread out and connected around the world. This is the kingdom we, as the followers of Christ, are at war with, and even though this dark kingdom is powerful in this world system, the Bible assure us that it is no match for the power of God that dwells within us!

"The incident at Babel and God's decision to disinherit the nations drew up the battle lines for a cosmic turf war for the planet. The corruption of the Elohim sons of God set over the nations meant Yahweh's vision of a global Eden would be met with divine force. Every inch outside of Israel would be contested, and Israel itself was fair game for hostile conquest. The gods would not surrender their inheritance back to Yahweh; He would have to reclaim them." ~ Michael Heiser

Through Paul's letter to the church at Corinth we can see idols represented demonic spirits. *"What am I trying to say? Am I saying that food offered to idols has some significance, or that idols are real gods? No, not at all. I am saying that these sacrifices are offered to demons, not to God. And I don't want you to participate with demons"* (1 Corinthians 10:19-20, NLT).

We also find the Lord instructing Israel to have nothing to do with the false gods of the people He was driving out of the Land which He was going to give to them. *"You shall not bow down to their gods, nor serve them, nor do according to their works; but you shall utterly overthrow them and completely break down their sacred pillars"* (Exodus 23:24, NKJ). Again the Scriptures say, "*When the LORD your God cuts off from before you the nations which you go to dispossess, and you displace them and dwell in their land, take heed to yourself that you are not ensnared to follow them, after they are destroyed from before you, and that you do not inquire after their gods, saying, 'How did these nations serve their gods? I also will do likewise'*" (Deuteronomy 12:29-30, NKJ).

It seems evident that these evil spiritual forces, which were geographically assigned, had set up evil practices in the lands they controlled that directly contradicted God's Law. *"According to the doings of the land of Egypt, where you dwelt, you shall not do; and according to the doings of the land of Canaan, where I am bringing you, you shall not do; nor shall you walk in their ordinances"* (Leviticus 18:3, NKJ).

Further evidence that evil spirits are geographically assigned can be found in the words of the Lord about the land of Egypt and its gods, (although there may be some who are not limited by geographical boundaries). *"For I will pass through the land of Egypt on that night, and will strike all the firstborn in the land of Egypt, both man and beast; and against all the gods of Egypt I will execute judgment: I am the LORD"* (Exodus 12:12, NKJ).

> *"Principalities do not merely possess power; they are power . . . pure power. . . capacity, dominion in person. . . these principalities exercise their being by taking possession of the world as a whole and of individual men, the elements, political and social institutions, historical conditions and circumstances, spiritual and religious trends.'* ~ Heinrich Schlier

With the understanding that evil spiritual forces occupy certain geographical territories, what conclusions can you come to about the area in which you currently reside?

_____

_____

_____

_____

What conclusion can we make about spiritual warfare and our task to advance the Kingdom of God, when we consider there are territorial spiritual forces?

_____

_____

_____

_____

Strong Holds

"The tools of our trade aren't for marketing or manipulation, but they are for demolishing that entire massively corrupt culture. We use our powerful God-tools for smashing warped philosophies, tearing down barriers erected against the truth of God, fitting every loose thought and emotion and impulse into the structure of life shaped by Christ." 2 Corinthians 10:4-5 (MSG)

Strong holds are old habits formed before we knew Jesus, or formed through times of walking in our flesh after we came to know Jesus. These strong holds (habits) are forms of behavior that believers are trapped in, realizing they are wrong, yet feeling powerless to escape. It's possible for a believer to truly be saved, and at the same time have an area of their life held captive by the enemy.

Strong holds are established by the adversary to hold people captive to Satan's will. These strong holds can be established through alcohol, sex, food, relationships, and drugs, to name just a few of the avenues the enemy may take in establishing strongholds in the lives of the children of God.

> *"Spiritual strongholds begin with a thought. One thought becomes a consideration. A consideration develops into an attitude, which leads then to action. Action repeated becomes a habit, and a habit establishes a 'power base for the enemy,' that is, a stronghold." Elisabeth Elliot*

The devil creates strongholds by tempting us to act in a sinful and addictive manner, which stimulates a sense of pleasure. These temptations, once acted on, create chemical reactions in the brain, which can create a sense of pleasure, security, or wellbeing.

Dopamine, which is a neurotransmitter, is one the chemicals released in the brain to stimulate pleasure. Dopamine helps to control the brain's reward and pleasure centers. It also helps regulate movement and emotional responses, and it enables us to not only see rewards, but to take action in moving toward them.

As we continue to act on the temptations the enemy entices us with the body builds up a tolerance to this pleasure causing chemical, and requires more of it to create the feeling of pleasure that is being sought after. The brain must continue to generate a larger amount of Dopamine, which in-turn creates a chemical dependency. This is the same as any drug addiction, making it difficult to break free from these sinful and destructive habits. This makes the strong hold both a spiritual battle and a physiological one.

It's important to note that strongholds can also be established by a lack of Dopamine being released in the brain, causing God's children to live in a constant state of fear and anxiety.

We must understand the brain is a physical organ that the enemy attacks to gain control over the children of God. These attacks keep them from living up to the fullest of their potential in Christ!

> *"If we exalt money, status, or sex above the Word of God, we are living in idolatry. Every time we inwardly submit to the strongholds of fear, bitterness, and pride, we are bowing to the rulers of darkness. Each of these idols must be smashed, splintered, and obliterated from the landscape of our hearts." ~ Francis Frangipane*

The Lord spoke to the children of Israel, through the Prophet Isaiah, saying, *"Listen to me, all you who are serious about right living and committed to seeking God. Ponder the rock from which you were cut, the quarry from which you were dug. Yes, ponder Abraham, your father, and Sarah, who bore you"* (Isaiah 51:1-2, MSG). If we are going to break strongholds in our lives we must first recognize what they are, but then we must also recognize who we are in Christ. We must understand that we have been cut from the eternal Rock, Jesus Christ!

New thoughts must be created by confessing with our mouth the way God sees us, regardless of our current action, so that we may gain a new image in our mind that correlates with God's Word concerning our new position with Him. The Bible reminds us of the power of our words, proclaiming, *"Wise words satisfy like a good meal; the right words bring satisfaction. The tongue can bring death or life; those who love to talk will reap the consequences"* (Proverbs 18:20-21, NLT).

Because there is a direct correlation between what we say and how our brain interprets reality, we can begin to create a new image of who we are, and at the same time begin to act and live in accordance with that new image!

Breaking strongholds is often NOT an overnight experience (although it indeed could be), but takes time and consistency in our efforts, under the power of the Holy Spirit, to establish a new image with new behavior patterns.

Breaking strongholds that have been held for years can often take the aid of another Christian, particularly one who is mature in the Lord, not a new believer. The Scriptures admonish us to help restore our brothers and sisters! *"Dear brothers and sisters, if another believer is overcome by some sin, you who are godly should gently and humbly help that person back onto the right path. And be careful not to fall into the same temptation yourself"* (Galatians 6:1, NLT). They also say, *"As iron sharpens iron, so one person sharpens another"* (Proverbs 27:17, NIV).

How can you recognize a stronghold in your life?

_____

_____

_____

_____

As you examine your life, if you see a stronghold the enemy has set up, what are some beginning steps you could take to break that stronghold?

_____

_____

_____

_____

Describe your attitude towards helping someone else who is being held captive by the enemy in a certain part of their life. What areas of sin/captivity would you have trouble helping another Believer to be set free? Why?

_____

_____

_____

_____

Godly Strong Holds

"Now when Daniel knew that the writing was signed, he went home. And in his upper room, with his windows open toward Jerusalem, he knelt down on his knees three times that day, and prayed and gave thanks before his God, as was his custom since early days." Daniel 6:10 (NKJ)

Daniel had developed a custom, or habit, of praying three times a day. This habit had nothing to do with how he felt, or even what was going through his mind daily, but everything to do with a conditioned response to being alive that day. This custom, or habit, was a godly stronghold that had been built up in his life; a stronghold that would help to ensure his success in Babylon.

When old evil strongholds are torn down in our lives new godly ones must be established in their place. If we merely tear down old strongholds and never build new ones for the Lord, we can be certain the enemy will be back, and prepared to build an even stronger-hold in that area of our life! *"When an evil spirit leaves a person, it goes into the desert, searching for rest. But when it finds none, it says, 'I will return to the person I came from.' So it returns and finds that its former home is all swept and in order. Then the spirit finds seven other spirits more evil than itself, and they all enter the person and live there. And so that person is worse off than before"* (Luke 11:24-26, NLT).

> *"Holiness is the habit of being of one mind with God, according as we find His mind described in Scripture. It is the habit of agreeing in God's judgment, hating what He hates, loving what He loves, and measuring everything in this world by the standard of His Word."*
> ~ J.C. Ryle

Godly strongholds can be created in our lives through disciplined daily activities, under the power of the Holy Spirit. These disciplined activities done over a period of time can develop into godly strongholds in our lives.

To be effective in the expansion of God's Kingdom we're going to have to have godly strongholds, fortified places in our lives, which the enemy cannot break through with its deceptive works of destruction.

"When we dare to depend entirely upon God and do not doubt, the humblest and feeblest agencies will become mighty through God, to the pulling down of strongholds." ~ A.B. Simpson

Habits of daily prayer, reading the Bible, and speaking God's Word over negative and distressing situations are some of the godly strongholds that should be developed in our lives! These habits will help to secure our success in the Mission we have been entrusted with!

What are some godly strongholds (habits) that need to be established in your life?

_____

_____

_____

_____

Of the strongholds (habits) you listed, pick one, and then list at least three steps you could take to start building that stronghold up in your life.

_____

_____

_____

_____

Chapter 5

The Enemy's Power

"Then the man who had the evil spirit jumped on them and overpowered them all. He gave them such a beating that they ran out of the house naked and bleeding." Acts 19:6 (NIV)

The devil's power is real. It is used to hinder the advancement of our Lord's Kingdom, to destroy those God has redeemed to himself, and to deceive mankind, claiming their souls for eternal destruction.

In Acts 19 we see the enemy exerting tremendous power over non-believers. Evil spirits are able to exercise unusual physical strength through those they have possessed. Here we see a clear illustration of the enemy's power in the physical world we live in.

We also find the enemy successfully resisting the Apostle Paul, for a time, keeping him from going to Thessalonica. In his first letter to the Thessalonians the Apostle Paul said, *"For we wanted to come to you—certainly I, Paul, did, again and again—but Satan blocked our way"* (1 Thessalonians 2:18, NIV).

> *"The devil is no idle spirit, but a vagrant, runagate walker, that never rests in one place. The motive, cause, and main intention of his walking is to ruin man."* ~ Thomas Adams

The dark spiritual forces of Satan's kingdom have real power, and depending on where each spirt/demon falls in the hierarchy of Satan's kingdom will determine the power that entity will be able to exert. Remember, there is a hierarchy of spiritual resistance, which means there are different levels of power the forces of evil are able to operate under.

As children of God, representing His interest here in this life, we must understand the enemy's power is real, and that he is able to attack us with that power at some of our weakest and most vulnerable moments. The adversary may wait for what he considers an opportune time, or he may attack us when he feels threatened by our efforts to expand the Kingdom, or he may even attack us just to support his evil nature. Satan and his dark kingdom are truly adversaries to the children of God and mankind as a whole. It is their job to create chaos and cause destruction in our lives, which they are ever so eager and happy to do! The word Satan in the Old Testament can be translated as adversary, and that is a perfect depiction of who and what the forces of darkness are to the children of God who labor to expand their Lord's Kingdom; they are our adversaries!

Though the enemy exerts real power here on the earth, we need not fear him, for greater is He who is in us than he who is in the world! *"You are from God, little children, and you have conquered them, because the One who is in you is greater than the one who is in the world"* (1 John 4:4, HCSB).

> *"Put very simply, Satan's power in the world is everywhere. Yet wherever men and women walk in the Spirit, sensitive to the anointing they have from God, that power of his just evaporates. There is a line drawn by God, a boundary where by virtue of his own very presence Satan's writ does not run. Let God but occupy all the space himself, and what room is left for the evil one?"* ~ Watchman Nee

The enemy may have real power, but so does God, and His is greater in every way! God has delegated His power to us, so that we would be able to stand against all the attacks and power of the enemy! *"In conclusion, be strong in the Lord [draw your strength from Him and be empowered through your union with Him] and in the power of His [boundless] might. Put on the full armor of God [for His precepts are like the splendid armor of a heavily-armed soldier], so that you may be able to [successfully] stand up against all the schemes and the strategies and the deceits of the devil"* (Ephesians 6:10-11, AMP).

What is power?

_____

_____

_____

_____

Describe how you've witnessed the devil exert his power, whether successful or not, in your life?

_____

_____

_____

_____

Physical Affliction

"And this woman, a daughter of Abraham as she is, whom Satan has bound for eighteen long years, should she not have been released from this bond on the Sabbath day?" Luke 13:16 (NASB)

This woman, as a daughter of Abraham, would not be an outsider to the family of God, but a future citizen of Heaven. Still, even though she was a daughter of Abraham, we find the devil had physically afflicted her. But now with Jesus on the scene, her deliverance had arrived! After 18 years of being physically afflicted by Satan, she would be set free by the Son of God!

> *"God has often permitted demons to act on and in the bodies of men and women; and it is not improbable that the principal part of unaccountable and inexplicable disorders still come from the same source." ~ Adam Clark*

As we talk about the enemy, and his power to cause physical afflictions on the children of God, and the world at large, we must be careful to examine the Bible in a holistic manner to gain a true picture of His power to afflict, and our power to resist.

When God originally created Adam and Eve, He gave them authority to reign upon the earth. But, when Adam sinned he essentially surrendered his God given authority over to the adversary, who wasted no time in using that authority to cause death and destruction throughout the world. *"Nevertheless death reigned from Adam to Moses, even over them that had not sinned after the similitude of Adam's transgression, who is the figure of him that was to come*" (Romans 5:14, KJV).

But when Jesus showed up on the scene He brought the cure for all the sickness and death the enemy had afflicted the world with! *"That evening they brought to him many who were possessed with demons; and he cast out the spirits with a word, and cured all who were sick. This was to fulfill what had been spoken through the prophet Isaiah, 'He took our infirmities and bore our diseases.'"* (Matthew 8:16-17, NRSV).

The Scriptures are clear; Jesus took the infirmities and sickness of the world in His own body! He took our weakness and gave us His strength! His body was broken for us! Our healing has been fully provided through Jesus Christ! In the above verse, Matthew references the Prophet Isaiah, for it had been written that the Servant of God (that's Jesus) would come and deliver the world from sin and sickness. Isaiah wrote concerning Him, saying, *"Surely he has borne our infirmities and carried our diseases; yet we accounted him stricken, struck down by God, and afflicted. But he was wounded for our transgressions, crushed for our iniquities; upon him was the punishment that made us whole, and by his bruises we are healed"* (Isaiah 53:4-5, NRSV). Matthew's reference to the Prophet Isaiah makes it clear that the prophet was not merely talking in a figurative manner about out spiritual healing only, but also our physical healing. Jesus paid the price for it all!

He has not only provided for our physical and spiritual healing, but also with His death on the cross and His resurrection from the grave, He took back the authority that Adam had lost to Satan. This is why He announced to His followers, *"All authority in heaven and on earth has been given to me. Go therefore and make disciples of all nations...*" (Matthew 28:18-19, NRSV).

We are armed with the authority of Christ, which Adam had lost. We have the power of the Holy Spirit. We are able to go throughout the world, representing our Lord, and freeing those who have been physically afflicted by the devil, in the name of Jesus Christ our King!

> *"It is our privilege in the power of the Holy Ghost to loose the prisoners of Satan and to let the oppressed go free"* ~ Smith Wigglesworth

The enemy has real power to physically afflict mankind, but we now have a greater power, and the authority of Christ to exercise that power over all the destructive works of the devil!

The devil can cause sickness; he is free to do so if he goes unchallenged by the children of God! You have an authority that no prophet in the Old Testament ever had. You should not be afraid to exercise the authority and power you've been given, to bring an end to the treacherous works of the adversary amongst mankind!

Why is physical affliction so effective in stopping the children of God in the work they have been called to do?

_____

_____

_____

_____

Why are many Christians hesitant in exercising the authority over sickness they have been given?

_____

_____

_____

_____

How can you be more effective in destroying the works of the devil, and bringing the healing Jesus has provided for all those who are afflicted physically to the world around you?

_____

_____

_____

_____

Emotional Affliction

"Be angry and do not sin. Don't let the sun go down on your anger, and don't give the Devil an opportunity." Ephesians 4:26-27 (HCSB)

Another way the enemy may afflict us is through our emotions. The devil has the ability to play on our emotions stirring up anger, jealousy, lust, grief, bitterness, regret, and anxiety, to name just a few.

Our emotions have been given to us by God as part of our being, and are intended to be subject to our New Nature, which is subject to the Holy Spirit. The devil attempts to gain power of our emotions, so he can use them to gain control over us.

The enemy knows if he can keep the child of God tied up with grief, lust, anger, or some other form of emotional bondage, he can make them of no effect in the war between *good* and *evil*.

Our emotions must remain bridled, under the control of our New Nature, which is led by the Spirit of God.

> *"No form of vice, not worldliness, not greed of gold, not drunkenness itself, does more to un-Christianize society than evil temper." ~ Henry Drummond*

The use of anger to gain control of God's children is such an effective strategy for the enemy because anger can come on quickly with little to no warning, and it moves the child of God to behave completely opposite of their identity in Christ.

Now, there is a godly anger that can move God's children as well, but be sure, the enemy wants no part of that, for this anger is always directed towards him and his works of destruction.

> *"By the anxieties and worries of this life Satan tries to dull man's heart and make a dwelling for himself there." ~ Francis of Assisi*

Our emotions are to be a powerful ally in the struggle against Satan and his demonic forces! Our emotions move us to live and act with passion for the Kingdom of God's sake! They move us to demonstrate God's love to the world around us. And, godly anger, which is directed at the enemy, and under the control of our New Nature, moves us to act courageously, free of fear and anxiety, regardless of the challenges that may lie ahead of us!

When we understand how powerful our emotions are in determining our response towards the world around us, it is easy to see why the enemy would afflict us emotionally.

Describe the power of your emotions to maneuver you in life?

_____

_____

_____

_____

How might the devil manipulate things around you to trigger an emotional response, so that he can gain a foothold in your life?

_____

_____

_____

_____

What steps can you take to ensure your emotions are kept under the care of your New Nature, while guarding them against the evil ploys of the enemy?

_____

_____

_____

_____

Family Affliction

"A Gentile woman who lived there came to him, pleading, 'Have mercy on me, O Lord, Son of David! For my daughter is possessed by a demon that torments her severely.'"
Matthew 15:22 (NLT)

This Gentile woman in the passage above was afflicted by an indirect attack of the enemy; he did not come after her, but her daughter, which caused her great distress. In fact, the distress was so great, it moved this Gentile woman to seek the aid of a Jewish man. It also moved her to humble herself before Jesus and His followers to a degree that may have seemed disgraceful to many of her fellow Gentiles.

If the devil cannot get to us directly, he may very well try an indirect approach by attacking our family members, which can even be more damaging to us emotionally than if he would have attacked us straight on. Because the devil is not above attacking our children, through any means he can, we must be vigilant in our efforts to guard them physically, emotionally, mentally, and spiritually against all of his schemes.

*"Every one of our children will be brought into the ark,
if we pray and work earnestly for them." D.L. Moody*

Realizing we are in a war, and that the enemy is looking for an opportunity to attack us and our family, we should endeavor to follow the Lord and His Word, refusing to go astray, not giving the devil an opportunity to step into our house and afflict our family!

We must set a good example for our children to follow, as we teach them the way in which they should go. If our actions don't match up with our words the enemy will surely take full advantage of the situation to lead our children astray and afflict them to the fullest of his evil potential!

*"Not to walk in the straight and narrow way yourself, is
to give the devil the biggest kind of a chance to get our
children." ~ Billy Sunday*

The war we are involved in with Satan and his demonic horde is real! And the enemy faces no moral dilemmas when it comes to afflicting our children; we must guard them, and teach them how to fight in the war! If we refuse to teach them about this spiritual war they are in, we set them up to be easy targets for the enemy! On the other hand, if we teach our children who they are in Christ, and how to fight the enemy, we not only give them a firm foundation to live in victory over the enemy, but we also give them the ability to be great leaders in the war between *good* and *evil*! *"Behold, children are a heritage from the LORD, The fruit of the womb is a reward. Like arrows in the hand of a warrior, so are the children of one's youth. Happy is the man who has his quiver full of them; they shall not be ashamed, But shall speak with their enemies in the gate"* (Psalm 127:3-5, NKJ).

"If you want to drive the devil out of the world, hit him with a cradle instead of a crutch." ~ Billy Sunday

Why would the enemy attack your children instead of directly attacking you?

_____

_____

_____

_____

What steps can you take to close the door to the attacks by the enemy on your home and children?

_____

_____

_____

_____

Financial Affliction

"For the love of money is the root of all kinds of evil. And some people, craving money, have wandered from the true faith and pierced themselves with many sorrows." 1 Timothy 6:10 (NLT)

Money is not evil; it is the love of money from which evil springs forth. But in truth, when we love anything above our God, evil has an opportunity to arise.

Since we currently reside in a physical world that uses a tangible currency, we will find it useful, and even needful in most cases. Having an adequate supply of this worlds currency, as we set out to advance the Kingdom of our Lord, can help to ensure things go much smoother than if we had a financial lack.

There is no shame in having an ample supply of finances at our disposal to advance the Kingdom with, as long as it is used wisely, and never makes its way to our hearts.

> *"Water is useful to the ship and helps it to sail better to the haven, but let the water get into the ship, if it is not pumped out, it drowns the ship. So riches are useful and convenient for our passage. We sail more comfortably with them through the troubles of this world; but if the water gets into the ship, if love of riches gets into the heart, then we are drowned by them."* ~ *Thomas Watson*

The enemy has the ability to afflict us financially in their attempts to draw our affection and trust away from God.

In natural warfare, one strategy the enemy would employ, as soon as the opportunity arose, would be that of cutting off the supply line of the opposing force. The devil, in his efforts to destroy us, will often times try to cut off our financial supply, tempting us to doubt God's ability to provide as He has promised. It has been said, *The devil comes where the money is; where it is not he comes twice.*

The devil may be able to block our financial supply, but he can only do it temporarily, if he catches us off guard. We must trust in the promises of God and the finished work of Jesus Christ to justify us, so that we may freely receive the promises of the righteous! We can be certain that God will provide for us financially! We simply need to keep our eyes on Him, trusting Him to fulfill all He has promised!

"What I'm trying to do here is to get you to relax, to not be so preoccupied with getting, so you can respond to God's giving. People who don't know God and the way he works fuss over these things, but you know both God and how he works. Steep your life in God-reality, God-initiative, God-provisions. Don't worry about missing out. You'll find all your everyday human concerns will be met" (Matthew 6:31-33, MSG).

"And this same God who takes care of me will supply all your needs from his glorious riches, which have been given to us in Christ Jesus" (Philippians 4:19, NLT).

The devil will surely try to afflict you financially, for this reason you must maintain a healthy attitude towards money. You should never love money, nor should you fear it. You should embrace the financial blessings you have through Christ, and wisely use those blessings to advance the Kingdom of your Lord!

> *"If a person gets his attitude toward money straight, it will help straighten out almost every other area in his life."~ Billy Graham*

How have you witnessed the devil attempt to financially afflict you in the past? And how did it turn out?

_____

_____

_____

_____

Why does the thought of money scare many Christians?

_____

_____

_____

_____

How does the lack of money limit many Christians?

_____

_____

_____

_____

How can you guard your heart when the devil comes after your financial supply?

_____

_____

_____

_____

How do you feel about God blessing you financially?

_____

_____

_____

_____

Chapter 6

The Father of Lies

"You are of your father the devil, and you want to do the desires of your father. He was a murderer from the beginning, and does not stand in the truth because there is no truth in him. Whenever he speaks a lie, he speaks from his own nature, for he is a liar and the father of lies." John 8:44 (NASB)

The ability to lie began with Satan! The enemy of our souls gave birth to the first lie! And, he has successfully used them to propagate his destructive works amongst mankind from the beginning.

A lie is a destructive force that attacks the righteousness of truth. It has the desire to destroy faith, and in doing so creates a platform of fear from which the enemy can establish a work of destruction in our lives!

Through the use of lies, Satan and the evil spiritual forces of his dark kingdom, have been able to take the truth of God's Word and manipulate it for their own destructive purposes! They twist scripture and use half-truths to deceive God's children into buying into their lies, giving them power over the lives of God's children.

> *"The devil can counterfeit all the saving operations and graces of the Spirit of God." ~ Johnathan Edwards*

As the father of lies, the enemy is a master of counterfeiting the works of God, deceiving mankind, and trapping them in his deceitful lies.

As the children of God, we must learn to measure everything off God's Word; understanding the New Covenant which we live under by faith through Jesus Christ!

The unabated truth of God's eternal Word is the only thing that can crush the lies of the enemy! It halts the destructive work he so longs to bring to the life of the child of God! God's Word not only destroys the lies of the enemy, but it creates an atmosphere of faith in which the blessings and promises of God can be freely and fully received by the believer!

> *"There are two equal and opposite errors into which our race can fall about the devils. One is to disbelieve in their existence. The other is to believe, and to feel an excessive and unhealthy interest in them. They themselves are equally pleased by both errors, and hail a materialist and a magician with the same delight."* ~ *C.S. Lewis*

One of the greatest lies the devil has perpetrated amongst mankind is the delusion of his existence and works. Through this lie the enemy has been able to masquerade himself as *"natural-occurrences"*, *"chance happenings"*, *"bad-luck"*, *"miss-fortune"*, *"fate"*, and *"God's mysterious workings"*; to name a few of his masquerades!

To combat the enemy, we must recognize the enemy! We must be able to distinguish between God's footprint and the devil's footprint! Jesus said, *"The thief comes only in order to steal and kill and destroy. I came that they may have and enjoy life, and have it in abundance [to the full, till it overflows]"* (John 10:10, AMP).

Always remember, the devil is a liar, and if you believe the liar you empower the liar! Don't believe the liar! Refuse to give the liar power over your life!

Describe how a lie causes destruction in the believer's life?

_____

_____

_____

_____

How has the use of lies strengthened the enemy's hold on mankind?

_____

_____

_____

_____

Twisted Scriptures

"Then the devil took him to Jerusalem, to the highest point of the Temple, and said, 'If you are the Son of God, jump off!' For the Scriptures say, 'He will order his angels to protect and guard you. And they will hold you up with their hands so you won't even hurt your foot on a stone.'" Luke 4:9-11 (NLT)

The devil is a master of taking the Scripture and putting an ever so slight of twist upon them to manipulate their righteous intent for his evil purpose!

The enemy attempts to twist the Scriptures, while endeavoring to deceive the follower of Christ. He doesn't change the wording, for that would be too obvious. No, he is much more clever than that. The enemy doesn't change the wording, but the meaning. By leaving the Scripture intact with its original syntax the enemy is better able to manipulate the child of God by changing the original intent of the Scriptures and putting his evil twist on them.

Satan is so confident in his knowledge of the Scriptures and ability to twist them that he attempted to do so even on Jesus! Satan took the Scripture and quoted it correctly, but used it out of context, and in a manner that directly contended with other Scriptures. Unfortunate for him, Jesus was the living Word and understood the written Scripture perfectly, and was able to rightly divide the Word of truth!

> *"The devil is a better theologian than any of us and is a devil still." ~ A.W. Tozer*

Your adversary knows the Bible, so if you are going to successfully confront him and overcome him, you must know the Word also. This means you must spend time, under the tutelage of the Holy Spirit, studying the Holy Scripture! *"Be diligent to present yourself approved to God, a worker who does not need to be ashamed, rightly dividing the word of truth"* (2 Timothy 2:15, NKJV).

Jesus was able to overcome the enemy by correctly dividing the truth of the Scriptures from the lying manipulative twist the enemy had placed on them!

> *"Satan tempts to sin under a pretense of religion. He is most to be feared when he transforms himself into an angel of light. He came to Christ with Scripture in his mouth: 'It is written.' The devil baits his hook with religion." ~ Thomas Watson*

If the Church of Jesus Christ is going to be successful at destroying the lies of the enemy, confronting the manipulating twist, which he loves to put on the Scriptures, it is going to have to learn to stand firm on the Word of God, refusing to compromise, and dividing the truth of God's Eternal Word from the manipulations of the enemy!

Why does the devil try to twist the Scripture, instead of directly contending with them when he is dealing with God's children?

_____

_____

_____

_____

How have you seen the devil attempt to twist the Scriptures when trying to gain a foothold in your life?

_____

_____

_____

_____

Was he successful in his attempts? Why or why not?

_____

_____

_____

_____

What are at least three steps you can take right away to ensure the enemy is unsuccessful in his attempts to twist the Scriptures in your eyes?

_____

_____

_____

_____

Half Truths

"Whatever I command you, be careful to observe it; you shall not add to it nor take away from it." Deuteronomy 12:32 (NKJ)

Half-truths are another of the devil's favorite ways of deceiving the followers of Christ. Half-truths are in truth, nothing more than lies. For to omit part of the truth, or to add a deception to a truth is to change said truth into a lie!

The greatest danger of a half-truth is the fact that it contains a partial truth. A truth that has been manipulated by the enemy in such a way as to deceive the believer and gain control over them.

> *"Whatever is only almost true is quite false, and among the most dangerous of errors, because being so near truth, it is the more likely to lead astray." ~ Henry Ward Beecher*

Some examples of half-truths the devil has successfully deployed upon many believers would be:

1. **You can't judge**: The Bible says, *"Judge not, that you be not judged."* This section of Scripture is found in Matthew and has been used by the enemy to keep God's children from making vital judgements about the people they are involved with. This is indeed only a half truth, for the entire seventh chapter of Matthew is about making judgments. In chapter seven of Matthew's Gospel it is clear that if we are doing the same thing as others we are not fit to judge. Judging for a Christian is not about condemning, but about helping, if at all possible. *"Or how can you say to your brother, 'Let me*

remove the speck from your eye'; and look, a plank is in your own eye? Hypocrite! First remove the plank from your own eye, and then you will see clearly to remove the speck from your brother's eye" (Matthew 7:4-5, NKJV). Jesus even goes on to say, *"Do not give what is holy to the dogs; nor cast your pearls before swine, lest they trample them under their feet, and turn and tear you in pieces"* (Matthew 7:6, NKJV). If the devil can keep God's children from making clear judgments, based off the truth of Scripture and led by the Holy Spirit, he can bring destruction and havoc to their lives.

2. **Resist the devil and he will eventually leave**: In the book of James the Bible clearly says, *"Resist the devil and he will flee from you."* This is true, but only a half-truth; for it also says, *"submit to God."* The devil knows we can resist him all we want, but if we are not submitted to God he's not going anywhere! This half-truth, which is again nothing more than a lie, has caused great confusion in the lives of many believers. Many of God's children find themselves resisting the devil, but to no avail, for they have embraced a half-truth. Our lives must be submitted to God if we are going to successfully resist and overcome the devil!

"And then she understood the devilish cunning of the enemies' plan. By mixing a little truth with it they had made their lie far stronger." ~ C.S. Lewis (The Last Battle)

Beware the enemy's use of half-truths in your life! Examine the entirety of God's Word, in the context it was intended, as you apply it to your life.

What half-truths has the enemy tried to inject into your life? And was he successful?

_____

_____

_____

_____

Describe the dangers of half-truths?

_____

_____

_____

_____

The Power of Agreement

"Beware lest any man spoil you through philosophy and vain deceit, after the tradition of men, after the rudiments of the world, and not after Christ." Colossians 2:8 (KJV)

If you believe a liar you empower the liar! In other words, if we believe the lies of the enemy we give him power over our lives.

When we come into agreement with the lies of the devil concerning our health, children, spouse, finances, or our purpose in life, we give him power over that area of our life! And that lie which the enemy has perpetrated begins to manifest into a living reality!

Jesus confirmed the power of agreement when He said, "*I also tell you this: If two of you agree here on earth concerning anything you ask, my Father in heaven will do it for you*" (Matthew 18:19, NLT).

Jesus also told a blind man who sought Him for healing, "*According to your faith let it be to you*" (Matthew 9:29, NKJV).

Just as prayer is about coming into agreement with the Word of God, so the devil understands that if he can get the child of God to come into agreement with one of his lies, they will eventually act on it, and that lie will manifest as a reality in their life.

> "*Show me a liar, and I will show thee a thief.*" ~ George Herbert

The devil is indeed both a liar and a thief! If he can get the child of God to believe one of his lies he can gain a foothold in their life, so that he may steal all the promises, the blessing, the goodness, and the great purpose God has planned for their life!

The child of God must embrace the Word of God as absolute truth, regardless of their presiding circumstances! At the same time we must reject the lies of the enemy, looking for the Lord to manifest His Word in our lives in due season!

God's Word is able to destroy all the lies of the enemy! We must use the Word as a hammer to do such! "*Is not My word like a fire? says the LORD, And like a hammer that breaks the rock in pieces*" (Jeremiah 23:29, NKJV)?

"A sacred regard to the authority of God ought to lead us to reject an error, however old, sanctioned by whatever authority, or however generally practiced." ~ Charles Spurgeon

If you can learn to reject the enemy's lies and come into agreement with the Word of God, you will see the power of God unleashed in your life like never before! And, at the same time you will see the chains the devil has used to control you and steal your Kingdom potential forever!

How does coming in agreement with an idea, whether from the enemy or our Lord, affect our reality?

_____

_____

_____

_____

How do we come into agreement with God and stay there?

_____

_____

_____

_____

Describe the power of agreeing with God's Word, and the captivity experienced when believers come into agreement with either a man centered idea or a demonic centered idea.

_____

_____

_____

_____

Chapter 7

The Enemy's Target

"So letting your sinful nature control your mind leads to death. But letting the Spirit control your mind leads to life and peace." Romans 8:6 (NLT)

The Holy Spirit and the devil battle for control over our mind. The Holy Spirit works through our **_new_** God given nature and the devil works through our **_old_** fallen nature. The mind is the target of the devil's assault on us. He knows if he can gain control of our mind through our Old Nature he will be able to control our lives.

The adversary tries to flood our mind with sinful thoughts of doubt and fear, leading us into paths of destruction, robbing us of our God given potential in Christ!

The Holy Spirit desires to fill our mind with the promises and goodness of God, inspiring love and faith, bringing us to a place where we realize the fullness of our potential in Christ!

> *"Various are the pleas and arguments which men of corrupt minds frequently urge against yielding obedience to the just and holy commands of God."* ~ *George Whitefield*

Our Old Nature and New Nature are like oil and water, they just don't mix!

Our New Nature yields to the truth of God's Word, and reaps the benefits of a life of Grace, lived through faith!

Our Old Nature questions the validity of God's Word. Its very nature is to rebel against God and His Word, and will always seek to do such. It will always find an excuse to justify itself in doing so.

The mind is the steering wheel, and either our Old Nature or our New Nature will do the steering! One steers towards life and the other towards death!

> *"Not until we have become humble and teachable, standing in awe of God's holiness and sovereignty. Acknowledging our own littleness, distrusting our own thoughts, and willing to have our minds turned upside down, can divine wisdom become ours." ~ J.I. Packer*

Our minds must indeed be turned upside down once we are saved, so that Christ may take control! Then we will be able to say as the Apostle Paul did when he wrote to the church in Galatia, *"I have been crucified with Christ; it is no longer I who live, but Christ lives in me; and the life which I now live in the flesh I live by faith in the Son of God, who loved me and gave Himself for me"* (Galatians 2:20, NKJ).

How have you experienced the enemy attacking your mind?

_____

_____

_____

_____

Why do you feel the mind is such a sought-after prize by the enemy?

_____

_____

_____

_____

How can you perceive when your Old Nature is controlling your mind, verses when your New Nature is in control? And is there anything you can do to ensure your New Nature stays at the wheel?

_____

_____

_____

_____

A Transformed Life

"Do not conform to the pattern of this world, but be transformed by the renewing of your mind. Then you will be able to test and approve what God's will is—his good, pleasing and perfect will." Romans 12:2 (NIV)

A renewed mind brings a transformed life! Until our mind is renewed we will never be able to experience the fullness of God's love and power towards us, nor will we be able to demonstrate such before the world. The enemy is very much aware of this truth, and so he does all he can to keep us conformed to our old thinking patterns.

It's interesting to note the word *"transformed"* is the Greek word *"metamorphoo"* from which we get the word *"metamorphosis"* which can be defined as, *"a change of the form or nature of a thing or person into a completely different one, by natural or supernatural means."* It is also the exact same word used to describe Jesus when He was *"transfigured"*. The Bible says:

> *"Now after six days Jesus took Peter, James, and John his brother, led them up on a high mountain by themselves; and He was transfigured (**metamorphoo**) before them. His face shone like the sun, and His clothes became as white as the light. And behold, Moses and Elijah appeared to them, talking with Him"* (Matthew 17:1-3, NKJV).

Jesus was supernaturally transformed before He could experience this heavenly wonder on planet earth. In the same way, your mind must be supernaturally renewed so that you may undergo a metamorphosis, being totally transformed, if you're going to experience the fullness of your Father's heavenly blessings and power here in this life!

What you think, and how you think, makes the difference between victory and defeat! God wants you to live in victory and therefore calls for your minds to be renewed so that your entire life may be transformed!

> *"The condition of an enlightened mind is a surrendered heart."* ~ Alan Redpath

For your mind to be renewed, your heart (which is your affectionate longings and desires) must be for the Lord alone; you must be completely surrendered to Him! It is only in the presence of our Lord that a resonating peace can be found that allows our minds the opportunity to rest, so that they may be supernaturally renewed.

The Apostle Paul wrote, *"Let the Spirit renew your thoughts and attitudes"* (Ephesians 4:23, NLT). The word *"let"* indicates that you must make a choice to allow the Spirit of God to move in your life, changing the way you view and perceive the realities around you! You must come into agreement with the Spirit of God as He reshapes the way you think, and the choices you make, bringing everything into agreement with the Word of God!

> *"Renewing the mind is a little like refinishing furniture. It is a two-stage process. It involves taking off the old and replacing it with the new. The old is the lies you have learned to tell or were taught by those around you; it is the attitudes and ideas that have become a part of your thinking but do not reflect reality. The new is the truth. To renew your mind is to involve yourself in the process of allowing God to bring to the surface the lies you have mistakenly accepted and replace them with truth. To the degree that you do this, your behaviour will be transformed."* ~ Charles Spurgeon

Once our minds are renewed, not only will our behavior be transformed, but our entire life! How we understand the power and promises of God, and our ability to partake freely of them will be completely changed! We will understand the position we hold in Jesus Christ, and the grace afforded to us through the New Covenant we now stand in!

A transformed life that exerts authority and power over the enemy, and displays the wondrous promises and miracles of God, starts with a renewed mind! This is why the enemy will do all he can to keep God's children conformed to the thinking patterns of this world, so that the will of God cannot be proved to those hearing the Gospel preached!

What does it mean to you to have your mind renewed?

_____

_____

_____

_____

What hinders you from having your life fully transformed by the renewing of your mind?

_____

_____

_____

_____

How can this hindrance be overcome?

_____

_____

What is a practical step you could take to overcome this hindrance?

_____

_____

_____

_____

The Gatekeeper

"For as he thinks in his heart, so is he…" Proverbs 23:7 (NKJ)

The word *"think"* used here is the Hebrew word *"sha`ar"* meaning *"to act as gate-keeper"*. Our thoughts can literally act as a gatekeeper, which opens us up to receive the blessing, promises, and power of God, or that closes us off from receiving them all!

Our thoughts are directly linked to the manifestation of God's will in our lives! This is why the enemy tries with all diligence to pollute our minds with thoughts of fear over what tomorrow may hold, doubts of whether God will fulfill the promises He has spoken to our hearts and through His written word. The enemy uses feelings of anxiety, desires for illicit sex, and every negative thought that directly and indirectly contradicts the eternal Word of God!

"All the great temptations appear first in the region of the mind and can be fought and conquered there. We have been given the power to close the door of the mind. We can lose this power through disuse or increase it by use, by the daily discipline of the inner man in things which seem small and by reliance upon the word of the Spirit of truth. It is God that worketh in you, both to will and to do of His good pleasure. It is as though He said, 'Learn to live in your will, not in your feelings.'" ~ Amy Carmichael

The Spirit of God works through our New Nature to control our thoughts, releasing the blessings and promises of God!

The enemy works through our Old Nature to infuse our mind with negative and sinful thoughts, blocking God's promises and blessing from manifesting in our lives, in-turn creating disappointment and resentment.

"The vision that you glorify in your mind, the ideal that you enthrone in your heart - this you will build your life by, this you will become." ~ James Allen

Our mind must be set on the promises and blessings of God! Our thoughts must continually be kept in check if we're going to live the life of victory in Christ we are called to live! *"And don't for a minute let this Book of The Revelation be out of mind. Ponder and meditate on it day and night, making sure you practice everything written in it. Then you'll get where you're going; then you'll succeed"* (Joshua 1:8, MSG).

We can't expect to live in victory over the devil if we allow him to run wild in our minds! We must continually speak God's truths over our lives, keeping our minds focused on our

Lord and His Word! In doing this we will be confronting the enemy's lies and attempts to gain control over our thoughts!

In what ways have you found your thoughts directing your life?

_____

_____

_____

_____

How can you be sure your thoughts serve to open the gate that will lead you to receiving the promises and blessings of God?

_____

_____

_____

_____

How has the enemy used your Old Nature to poison your thoughts and steal your blessings?

_____

_____

_____

_____

Choosing Your Thoughts

"Summing it all up, friends, I'd say you'll do best by filling your minds and meditating on things true, noble, reputable, authentic, compelling, gracious—the best, not the worst; the beautiful, not the ugly; things to praise, not things to curse."
Philippians 4:8 (MSG)

The Bible is clear; the way we think matters! Our thought life is not something we can afford to take for granted if we're going to live up to the fullest of our potential in Jesus Christ, and experience all the grace and mercy God has so richly provided for us through our Lord and Savior!

We must learn to measure every thought, taking no part of our thought life for granted!

Question your thoughts! Is your thinking right? Do you have accurate thinking about how God works?

We have the ability to change our thoughts; to change the way we think about God, and how He works!

The devil wants to keep us believing lies, to deceive us about the way God really works. For if he can do this he can keep us from living in the fullness of God's goodness and mercy; he can keep us from receiving the blessings of God.

Recognize how God works! If your thinking about what you believe God is doing in your life doesn't line up with what the Bible says, then you must change the way you think.

Remember what side of the cross you are living on, and know it makes all the difference in the world!

"The object of opening the mind, as of opening the mouth, is to shut it again on something solid." ~ G.K. Chesterton

The Word of God is indeed solid! It never changes! We must fill our mind with God's Word, with the understanding that we are living under the New Covenant of God's Grace! We must maintain **RIGHT THINKING** about our relationship with God and how He works in our lives! For it is a relationship based off the finished work of Jesus Christ!

"Blessed [fortunate, prosperous, and favored by God] is the man who does not walk in the counsel of the wicked [following their advice and example], nor stand in the path of sinners, nor sit [down to rest] in the seat of scoffers (ridiculers). But his delight is in the law of the Lord, and on His law [His precepts and teachings] he [habitually] meditates day and night. And he will be like a tree firmly planted [and fed] by streams of water, which yields its fruit in its season; its leaf does not wither; and in whatever he does, he prospers [and comes to maturity]." Psalm 1:1-3 (AMP)

To live in the fullness of all God has for you, you must discipline your mind to think on the things of God! To focus on His promises and His goodness! To remember His testimonies! To reject every thought of fear, doubt, and perversion the enemy tries to inject into your mind, attempting to invade your thought life! Your thoughts must be consumed with your Lord, and His unfailing love and grace!

"He who loves will rejoice in the Truth, rejoice not in what he has been taught to believe; not in this Church's doctrine or in that; not in this issue, or in that issue; but "in the Truth. He will accept only what is real; he will strive to get at facts; he will search for Truth with a humble and unbiassed mind, and cherish whatever he finds at any sacrifice." ~ Henry Drummond

Understanding and embracing the truth of God's Word, regardless of what your circumstances may be, or what our eyes may see, will enable you to live in continuous victory over the enemy! And to experience the full measure of God's grace and goodness, which He desires to pour out on His children through Jesus Christ!

Turn around your thoughts:

1. Write down any thoughts about God and how He works that are currently influencing you?

2. Search the Scriptures to see if those thoughts are true from a New Covenant perspective.

3. Do your thoughts and the Scriptures match up without you having to add or take away from one or the other?

4. Rewrite your original thoughts and put them in line with the Scriptures and your New Covenant position of Grace, which you have by faith through Jesus Christ.

5. Begin to proclaim these new beliefs out loud, and continue to challenge any thoughts that would attempt to lead you away from this new way of thinking! Realize as you proclaim these biblical truths of God's Will towards you that there is a direct correlation between what you say and what your brain perceives as truth.

Chapter 8

Stumbling Stones

"Stay alert! Watch out for your great enemy, the devil. He prowls around like a roaring lion, looking for someone to devour." 1 Peter 5:8 (NLT)

Our enemy is a master manipulator and deceiver. He is cunning and crafty. He will use any means at his disposal to find a way to completely destroy us! The devil prays on the weaknesses of God's children, and those weaknesses vary with each individual soul.

All of God's children have weak points in their armor. They have areas in their life where they are more likely to fall or stumble than others. Wisdom would tell us to be aware of these areas, knowing full well the enemy will do all he can to exploit them.

We must endeavor to always stay alert, knowing the devil doesn't take holidays, and will joyfully exploit any weakness in our armor which we neglect to protect or strengthen!

> *"Satan, like a fisher, baits his hook according to the appetite of the fish." ~ Thomas Adams*

The enemy will use whatever ploy he deems suited to catch and destroy the children of God!

Whether pride, fear, sex, greed, doubt, or anger the enemy will strategically craft an individual plan for each of God's children to exploit their weakness (and in truth all of God's children have one...and if you feel you're the exception, check out pride). The enemy attempts to steal their God given potential, to destroy their life and the lives of their family members, to bring total chaos to them, to completely and totally devour them!

If you were the devil, what area of your life would you exploit?

_____

_____

_____

_____

If you were the devil, what strategy would you employ to attack your weakness?

_____

_____

_____

_____

Pride

"First pride, then the crash—the bigger the ego, the harder the fall." Proverbs 16:18 (MSG)

Pride is an exalted sense or awareness of one's own accomplishments or failures, both good and bad, which takes some form of gratification that can be experienced outwardly or held inwardly, by focusing on and lifting up those accomplishments and failures.

Pride is focused on *"self"*. It is occupied with *"I"* instead of the great *"I AM"*.

Pride is consumed with one's own achievements, as well as one's own sins.

It is the work of pride to turn our attention from Jesus, and all He has accomplished and suffered, to all we have achieved or had to endure.

Pride is deadly, and because of its self-preoccupation, it restricts believers from looking to Jesus and depending on His finished work on the cross to receive the full measure of God's grace.

Pride is a stumbling stone the enemy loves to use. It causes believers to crash and fall short of the grace God so eagerly desires to give them!

The devil skillfully wielded pride to attack Adam and Eve, causing them to fall from God's grace; missing out on all the goodness and blessings God desired to lavish upon them!

> *"There is nothing into which the heart of man so easily falls as pride, and yet there is no more vice which is more frequently, more emphatically, and more eloquently condemned in Scripture. Pride is a thing which should be unnatural to us, for we have nothing to be proud of. In almost every other sin, we gather us ashes when the fire is gone. But here, what is left? The covetous man has his shining gold, but what does the proud man have? He has less than he would have had without pride, and is no gainer whatever. Pride wins no crown."* ~ Charles Spurgeon

Pride spoils the hearts of men and women, turning them from God, allowing the enemy to control them through their Old Nature.

Pride is like a dividing wall that blocks the blessings of God from reaching the hands of His children, and humility is the hammer that breaks the wall to pieces! *"But He gives us more and more grace [through the power of the Holy Spirit to defy sin and live an obedient life that reflects both our faith and our gratitude for our salvation]. Therefore, it says, 'God is opposed to the proud and haughty, but [continually] gives [the gift of] grace to the humble [who turn away from self-righteousness].' So submit to [the authority of] God. Resist the devil [stand firm against him] and he will flee from you"* (James 4:6-7, AMP).

> *"Self-righteousness is the devil's masterpiece to make us think well of ourselves."* ~ Thomas Adams

Stay alert to *"Unassuming Pride"* for it is perhaps the most dangerous of all! Unassuming Pride goes unnoticed by most Christians; it lies within our hearts and is never shouted out or proclaimed verbally, but stands tall within our hearts to prevent the grace of God from overwhelming us. Unassuming Pride is fixated with what it is capable of doing and what it has accomplished in the past. It has no problem giving God token credit verbally, but inside claims all the glory for *"self"*. Beware of Unassuming Pride in your heart, it keeps the fullness of God's blessing and promises at bay. It is ready to receive only what it feels it has *"earned"* and *"deserves"*.

Let Christ and His accomplishments be the focus of your attention! Make a choice to put all your trust and delight in the work of Jesus, and you will reap the benefits and blessings of His righteousness!

How would you define pride?

_____

_____

_____

_____

How has pride tripped you up in the past?

_____

_____

_____

_____

How can you keep pride in check and prevent the enemy from using it as a stumbling stone in your life?

_____

_____

_____

_____

Idleness

"Because of laziness the building decays, and through idleness of hands the house leaks." Ecclesiastes 10:18 (NKJ)

When a vehicle is idling, its engine is running, but the vehicle itself is not moving. The vehicle was designed to move. Although it is capable of standing still, it was not designed to do so, and will not fulfill its purpose for which it was created while sitting in an idle state.

God's children are much the same way, we were made to move! The devil isn't happy about our position in Christ, and knows he can do nothing to steal the salvation we have received from Jesus. So, he will do all he can to keep us from engaging in the war for the souls of mankind and the establishing Kingdom realties upon this earth as we are called to do.

As God's children, we were created anew to RUN! Our motor is continually running because the Holy Spirit is forever alive in us! But, if the enemy can get us sidetracked and confused about our purpose in life he can keep us idle, running but going nowhere!

"Idleness is the burial of a living man." ~ Jeremy Taylor

Whether it's sitting in front of a television or passing the time of day without thought or purpose, the enemy is always looking for ways to keep God's children from moving forward for the glory of Christ and expansion of His Kingdom!

The devil will use anything he can to keep us idle in the spiritual realm. He doesn't mind us being involved in the worldly realm of self-seeking ambitions and personal pursuits as long as we stay in an idle mode when it comes to the advancement of the Kingdom. The devil does not want us involved in our Father's affairs!

> *"The idle man is the devil's cushion, on which he taketh his free ease, who, as he is incapable of any good, so he is fitly disposed for all evil motions." ~ Joseph Hall*

The enemy wants to hold us down! Therefore we must stay alert, aware of his tactics, not allowing ourselves to fall over the stumbling stone of idleness!

One of the greatest dangers of idleness is that it usually happens to the believer without their knowledge. The devil is cunning enough to use idleness on a believer, intermingled with pride, to make the believer think he or she is doing nothing wrong by sitting still. The devil tells them they are justified in their idleness, they work hard and are busy with other important things, and someone with more time should be working to advance the Kingdom. Idleness keeps them from making any impact for the Kingdom of God, and achieving all the Lord has called them to do.

What does it mean to be idle in Kingdom warfare?

_____

_____

_____

_____

If the devil were going to use idleness to trip you up, how might he place this stone so that you would trip over it?

_____

_____

_____

_____

How has the enemy used idleness against the Church of Christ as a whole?

_____

_____

_____

_____

Fear

"There is no fear in love. But perfect love drives out fear, because fear has to do with punishment. The one who fears is not made perfect in love." 1 John 4:18 (NIV)

"*Fear Not*" appears more times than any other phrase in the Bible. It seems obvious that God is trying to get something across to us!

God is perfect love and operates in that love. On the other side of the coin we find fear and Satan. As God uses love to minister to His children, the enemy uses fear to control and hold captive the child of God.

Fear is very much like a ball and chain that holds the child of God back from the glorious destiny that their Heavenly Father has prepared for them.

When God's perfect love is allowed to infiltrate every part of our being, fear can no longer hold us back!

Fear doubts God's unconditional love, it doubts God's Word, it doubts God's ability and/or willingness to keep His promises; fear poisons the soul of the child of God.

When we fully understand our position with God, through Jesus Christ, love fills our being and at the same time vanquishes all fear! When the love of our Heavenly Father overcomes us we don't doubt His Word, His promises, or His unfailing, unconditional love! *"For I am persuaded, that neither death, nor life, nor angels, nor principalities, nor powers, nor things present, nor things to come, nor height, nor depth, nor any other creature, shall be able to separate us from the love of God, which is in Christ Jesus our Lord"* (Romans 8:38-39, KJV).

Love creates faith as fear creates doubt! Faith makes everything possible as doubt robs us of every possibility!

Fear is one of the enemy's favorite devices to use in causing the child of God to stumble, falling short of receiving the promises of God and the life of eternal significance their Father has prepared for them.

> *"Fear is born of Satan, and if we would only take time to think a moment we would see that everything Satan says is founded upon a falsehood."* ~ A.B. Simpson

We must learn to recognize the enemy's use of fear in our lives. God doesn't use fear to direct or lead His children; He does that by the Holy Spirit and His written Word.

The enemy on the other-hand, uses fear to control the child of God. The enemy creates doubt and anxiety, rendering the child of God helpless and useless for the purpose of the advancement of the Kingdom of their Lord, which they were created for!

> *"Any time we open ourselves up to fear, we fall prey to his deceptions and intimidations. Yet, if we submit our hearts to God and stand in faith, we can resist those first fearful thoughts. As we yield to God we can master our reactions to fear and the enemy will soon flee." ~ Francis Frangipane*

We have a choice whether we allow fear to have a spot in our hearts; we actually get to choose! Both fear and love are based off actions and not mere emotional content. So, when we allow the love of God to move within us, it always stirs us to action.

When Jesus had compassion on someone He was always moved to action! The same must hold true for us! When the enemy attacks us with fear, we get to choose whether we will act on that fear or not.

God has commanded us to be courageous! But we must understand that courage is not the absence of the emotional feeling of dread, but rather the refusal to act on that feeling!

Describe fear?

_____

_____

_____

_____

How has the enemy successfully used fear in the past to trip you up?

_____

_____

_____

_____

How can fear be overcome?

_____

_____

_____

_____

Condemnation

"So now there is no condemnation for those who belong to Christ Jesus. And because you belong to him, the power of the life-giving Spirit has freed you from the power of sin that leads to death." Romans 8:1-2 (NLT)

To condemn someone is to pass a judgement against them that brings a punishment of recompense for the crime committed. The Bible is clear, for those who are in Christ Jesus there can be no condemnation. That means no judgment can be passed against them; they can be convicted of no crime!

Far too many of God's children still look to Him in fear and dread, believing their Heavenly Father is out to get them every time they fall short of the mark. This couldn't be further from the truth! But it's an incredibly effective stumbling stone that the adversary uses to trip up the child of God, keeping them from experiencing the goodness and love of their Heavenly Father.

> *"The Devil accuses us when we fall, but he has not so much on his side as we have." ~ Stephen Charnock*

The fear of condemnation causes the child of God to run from their Father when they commit a sin, instead of running to Him. Consequently, because they stay away from Him, they continue to struggle with the same sins. God is not looking to punish His children, but to deliver them!

Jesus took our punishment and gave us His righteousness, which is why we are **FREELY** justified by **GRACE** when we believe on Christ, apart from anything we could ever do!

Read what the Bible declares:

"But he was pierced for our rebellion, crushed for our sins. He was beaten so we could be whole. He was whipped so we could be healed. All of us, like sheep, have strayed away. We have left God's paths to follow our own. Yet the Lord laid on him the sins of us all" (Isaiah 53:5-6, NLT).

"Yet God, in his grace, freely makes us right in his sight. He did this through Christ Jesus when he freed us from the penalty for our sins. For God presented Jesus as the sacrifice for sin. People are made right with God when they believe that Jesus sacrificed his life, shedding his blood. This sacrifice shows that God was being fair when he held back and did not punish those who sinned in times past, for he was looking ahead and including them in what he would do in this present time. God did this to demonstrate his righteousness, for he himself is fair and just, and he makes sinners right in his sight when they believe in Jesus" (Romans 3:24-26, NLT).

If we understand our position with God through Jesus Christ the devil will never be able to use condemnation to keep us away from our Father in Heaven, which in-turn means he cannot keep us trapped in habitual sin!

Remember that perfect love casts out all fear! Your Father in Heaven loves you with a perfect love, and He is not out to punish, hurt, or condemn you! Know you are perfectly loved!

> *"The work of redemption was accomplished by Christ in His death on the cross and has in view the payment of the price demanded by a holy God for the deliverance of the believer from the bondage and burden of sin. In redemption the sinner is set free from his condemnation and slavery to sin." ~ John F. Walvoord*

Keeping the Law never made anyone right with God, for no one was ever able to keep it all! Jesus is the only One to ever complete all the righteous requirements of the Law fully, which is why He was able to trade out our sin for His righteousness.

The Law is good, and was never the problem; the problem was our inability to keep it. Because God loves us so greatly He made a way for us to be justified apart from the righteous Law.

Jesus has completely freed us from the requirements of the Law, we are no longer under the Law, but under GRACE! We are dead to the Law, and have no Law to break; therefore we cannot be condemned according to the Law! *"For the law always brings punishment on those who try to obey it (The only way to avoid breaking the law is to have no law to break!)"* (Romans 4:15, NLT).

When we fully understand this, not only does the devil lose the false power of condemnation he enjoys using against us, but we gain the power of God to live lives free from the sinful acts that enslave this world! *"Oh, what a miserable person I am! Who will free me from this life that is dominated by sin and death? Thank God! The **ANSWER is in Jesus Christ our Lord**…"* (Romans 7:24-25, NLT).

Know that you are a child of privilege, no longer under the Law, freed from the curse! *"Because of our faith, Christ has brought us into this place of **undeserved privilege** where we now stand, and we confidently and joyfully look forward to sharing God's glory"* (Romans 5:2, NLT).

You are treasured and loved by God, so don't fear Him, run to Him! Your Father in Heaven is looking to bless you, not punish you! It's only in His presence that you will find fullness of joy!

How has the devil used condemnation in the past to keep you in sin and away from God?

_____

_____

_____

_____

How can you be sure to live in the freedom Christ has provided for you?

_____

_____

_____

_____

Chapter 9

Recognizing The Enemy

"After all, we don't want to unwittingly give Satan an opening for yet more mischief—we're not oblivious to his sly ways!" 2 Corinthians 2:11 (MSG)

Many Christian don't like to consider the reality of Satan and the work of his dark kingdom; they would rather live in a state of ignorance than to consider the truth of the demonic work that are ever present amongst mankind.

When it comes to Kingdom warfare ignorance is not bliss! Ignorance will lead to nothing but a life ravished by the destructive works of the enemy!

We must learn to recognize, and successfully confront, the workings of Satan and his demonic forces!

> *"Satan's arsenal consists of such things as fear, worry, doubt, and self-pity. Every one of these weapons robs us of peace and leaves us troubled inside. Do you want to discern where the enemy is coming against you? In the network of your relationships, wherever you do not have peace, you have war. Conversely, wherever you have victory, you have peace. When Satan hurls his darts against you, the more peace you have during adversity, the more truly you are walking in Christ's victory." ~ Francis Frangipane*

The enemy is a master of deception and lies, and uses them both to distort the truth of God's Word concerning our lives and circumstance, to create fear, worry, doubt, and self-pity, so that he may spur death and destruction in our lives!

In discerning the work of the enemy, we must understand how God works and how the enemy works. God doesn't use fear, worry, doubt, self-pity, or sickness to speak to us, or to move us to action. God speaks to us through the Holy Spirit and moves us using love, which breeds faith! If we don't know the difference between the two we can never successfully wage war against the enemy!

> *"I have heard people say that there are no demons or devils. . . . . the Devil surely will not reveal himself to people who do not believe ; for, should he do so, they might believe, and that would be against his own sly, diabolical policy, as he would have all in the dark, so terrible is his enmity against the Eternal Source of Light and Treasure of Goodness—God Almighty."* ~ *Sebastian Dabovich*

We can choose to live in blissful ignorance of Satan and his dark kingdom like frightened children hiding under their bed-covers at night. Or we can choose to look for and recognize his works, shining the light of Jesus Christ on them, bringing deliverance and restoration to this broken world and its people!

What is the work of the enemy?

_____

_____

_____

_____

How can you distinguish between the work of God in your life and the work of the enemy?

_____

_____

_____

_____

Try The Spirit

"Beloved, believe not every spirit, but try the spirits whether they are of God: because many false prophets are gone out into the world." 1 John 4:1 (KJV)

Jesus warns us that Satan appears as an angel of light, and so it should come as no surprise that his angels appear as ministers of light. For this reason, we must endeavor to try every spirit, and every situation, to see if it is of God or the enemy.

The stakes in this war are too high to take things at face value! We must not be afraid to make a judgement about the people we encounter or the situations we face. But in doing so we must try everything righteously, which means judging by using the Word of God as a measuring stick for everything, but always doing so under the guidance of the Holy Spirit.

> *"To discern spirits we must dwell with Him who is holy, and He will give the revelation and unveil the mask of satanic power on all lines." ~ Smith Wigglesworth*

There are times when everything looks right and sounds correct, as if it were surely in-line with the Word of God. But something inside us is uneasy, our spirit is not settled. Our spirit, which is in direct communion with the Holy Spirit, is able to discern from what is of God and what is not, regardless of how it may look or sound. We must become accustomed to listening to the Holy Spirit and staying alert to its promptings and guidance.

The Spirit is always ready to reveal the truth to us. We must make the choice to look to the Spirit for revelation, and not depend merely on our natural senses. Remember, *"We walk by faith, not by sight"* (2 Corinthians 5:7, NKJV).

It's not that our natural senses cannot be used in trying the spirit of a person, or any given situation, but that the revelation we receive from the Holy Spirit always trumps our natural senses!

> *"One of the most subtle burdens God ever puts on us as saints is this burden of discernment concerning other souls. He reveals things in order that we may take the burden of these souls before Him and form the mind of Christ about them. It is not that we bring God into touch with our minds, but that we rouse ourselves until God is able to convey His mind to us about the one for whom we intercede."* ~ Oswald Chambers

Try every spirit, taking nothing at face value, using the Word of God as a measuring stick for all truth and the Holy Spirit as the official interpreter of that truth, and the devil will not easily deceive you!

What does it mean to judge righteously?

_____

_____

_____

_____

Tell of a time when you faced a situation where everything
was not as it seemed. How did the Holy Spirit work in you
during that time?

_____

_____

_____

_____

When you consider the idea of "*trying the spirit*" what does
that look like to you personally?

_____

_____

_____

_____

Exercise Wisdom

"Get wisdom; develop good judgment. Don't forget my words or turn away from them." Proverbs 4:5 (NLT)

As we consider the things of monetary value that many seek after, seldom is wisdom included, yet the Bible declares, *"Wisdom is far more valuable than rubies. Nothing you desire can compare with it"* (Proverbs 8:11, NLT). Wisdom gives us the power to gain wealth! Not only does it give us the power to gain wealth, but it also gives us the ability to successfully engage the enemy in spiritual warfare!

Having the knowledge of how to fight the enemy is not the same as having the wisdom to apply that knowledge. We must have both if we are going to be successful in our efforts to overthrow the works of the devil in our lives and in the world around us!

Wisdom may be defined as the ability to take acquired knowledge and correctly apply it to any given situation, coupled with a righteous discernment of said situation.

Wisdom gives us the ability to fight the enemy in a productive manner, to use our resources and energy in a way that will most benefit the Kingdom of God!

> *"Wisdom is the power to see and the inclination to choose the best and highest goal, together with the surest means of attaining it." ~ J.I. Packer*

The wisdom that shows itself to be wiser than anything the enemy can produce comes only from the Lord, and is available to us upon request. *"If you need wisdom, ask our generous*

God, and he will give it to you. He will not rebuke you for asking" (James 1:5, NLT).

Attempting to combat the devil with our own understanding and discernment is a sure recipe for disaster!

> *"Where fear is present, wisdom cannot be." ~ Lucius Caecilius Firmianus Lactantius*

We must be aware of the enemy's use of fear to mislead us! When our hearts are flooded with fear and anxiety it is virtually impossible to receive wisdom from the Lord. For just as love always produces faith, fear always produces doubt in our hearts and minds, which in-turn causes us to waver in our attitude of faith towards God. The Bible declares, *"But when you ask him, be sure that your faith is in God alone. Do not waver, for a person with divided loyalty is as unsettled as a wave of the sea that is blown and tossed by the wind. Such people should not expect to receive anything from the Lord"* (James 1:6-7, NLT).

As we continue to cultivate our relationship with our Heavenly Father, spending time with Him, we can be sure our hearts will be filled with His love, which removes all fear. Then we will be free to receive the wisdom we need to successfully defeat the enemy every time! *"There is no fear in love [dread does not exist]. But perfect (complete, full-grown) love drives out fear, because fear involves [the expectation of divine] punishment, so the one who is afraid [of God's judgment] is not perfected in love [has not grown into a sufficient understanding of God's love]"* (1 John 4:18, AMP).

Why is wisdom so valuable?

_____

_____

_____

_____

How can you be sure to act with godly wisdom?

_____

_____

_____

_____

Stay Silent

"Even a fool is counted wise when he holds his peace; when he shuts his lips, he is considered perceptive." Proverbs 17:28 (NKJ)

Surely one of the characteristic that springs from wisdom is the ability to remain silent in times of crises and confusion when the enemy attacks.

Knowing the power our words carry, and the pure emotional outburst we are capable of, staying silent when we discern the work of the enemy in our lives is one of the best things we can do.

Holding our tongue gives us time to assess the situation, examining it in the light of God's eternal Word. It gives us the ability to respond accordingly with our words and actions, as we are led by the Spirit and not our flesh.

> *"Wise people say nothing in dangerous times." ~John Selden*

It is in our silence that God has an opportunity to speak, and we have the opportunity to listen.

The power of silent moments in the midst of the enemy's attack should not be overlooked!

Confusion often abounds when the enemy strikes, and in that confusion we often interpret things incorrectly, because our emotions are at a heightened level of stimulation. Therefore, silence is needed to discern the situation and the work of the enemy. For it is in the silence that we will find the voice of God speaking to our hearts, giving us understanding and wisdom on how we should respond, and the words we should speak!

The Prophet Elijah learned this lesson as his life was threatened and his emotions ran rapid. Elijah feared he was the only one left who remained loyal to the Lord. The Bible says:

> *"The Lord said, 'Go out and stand on the mountain in the presence of the Lord, for the Lord is about to pass by.' Then a great and powerful wind tore the mountains apart and shattered the rocks before the Lord, but the Lord was not in the wind. After the wind there was an earthquake, but the Lord was not in the earthquake. After the earthquake came a fire, but the Lord was not in the fire. And after the fire came a gentle whisper. When Elijah heard it, he pulled his cloak over his face*

*and went out and stood at the mouth of the cave. Then
a voice said to him, 'What are you doing here, Elijah?'"*
(1Kings 19:11-13, NIV).

Elijah learned, as we must, that it is in the stillness, and not the
chaos, which we will find the voice of the Lord giving us the
guidance we need to be victorious over any situation the enemy
may throw our way.

> *"Learn to hold thy tongue; five words cost Zacharias
> forty weeks of silence." ~ Thomas Fuller*

We can be certain that words spoken hastily in the heat of the
moment can be costly! When the enemy attacks, hold your
tongue and look to God to guide you in responding in a manner
that will bring you the victory!

Why is it so difficult for God's children to remain silent when
chaos breaks loose?

_____

_____

_____

_____

How does the enemy take advantage of our emotional
responses?

_____

_____

_____

_____

Chapter 10

All Authority

"Then Jesus came to them and said, 'All authority in heaven and on earth has been given to me.'" Matthew 28:18 (NIV)

Before Jesus leaves this world, He makes it clear to His followers that all authority had been given to Him, both on earth and in Heaven. The authority that God once gave to Adam and was lost to Satan had now been taken back by Jesus!

There is no power that exists in all of creation which must not yield to the authority of Jesus Christ! *"Therefore, God elevated him to the place of highest honor and gave him the name above all other names, that at the name of Jesus every knee should bow, in heaven and on earth and under the earth, and every tongue declare that Jesus Christ is Lord, to the glory of God the Father"* (Philippians 2:9-11, NLT).

The enemy still has power, but the authority he once held has been lost! Jesus reigns supreme! We must embrace this as an absolute truth, for Satan and his dark angels are masters of illusion. They have the ability to manipulate any situation to make it seem as though they have authority, and that God's Word is merely a subjective truth at best. Our enemy is indeed the father of lies!

Because Jesus has all authority in Heaven and upon earth, His word reigns as absolute! It trumps all the powers of the enemy; this is why he must use deception to gain control over us and our life circumstances!

We must never operate merely by what we see, but without hesitation, we must operate in unwavering faith, that moves in accordance with God's Word, regardless of the illusions the enemy may try to set before our natural eyes! Remember, Jesus is the living Word, and He has ALL authority!!

> *"In order for a war to be just, three things are necessary. First, the authority of the sovereign. Secondly, a just cause. Thirdly, a rightful intention." ~ Thomas Aquinas*

There must be no doubt of the continuous struggle between Light and Darkness, the forces of our Lord and the forces of Satan and his dark kingdom. Yet, in this struggle our Lord's authority is sovereign, His rule is absolute, we must never doubt this! The enemy's authority has been toppled, and soon his dark kingdom will be destroyed! As the end of the earthly ministry of Jesus draws to a climax, He tells His disciples, *"The time for judging this world has come, when Satan, the ruler of this world, will be cast out. And when I am lifted up from the earth, I will draw everyone to myself"* (John 12:31-32, NLT).

The judgment of this world and the casting down of Satan is certainly the language of war. Jesus made it clear to His followers what His intent was, He was not merely a sacrificial Lamb, but also a warrior King who was about to bring the forces of darkness to their knees. The Apostle Paul makes the victory of Jesus over the forces of darkness clear, saying, *"He canceled the record of the charges against us and took it away by nailing it to the cross. In this way, he disarmed the spiritual rulers and authorities. He shamed them publicly by his victory over them on the cross"* (Colossians 2:14-15, NLT).

Rodney Whitacre puts it well when he says, *"He has come into enemy-occupied territory, defeated the ruler who had usurped the region, revealed the true state of bondage that had existed under this false ruler and reclaimed it for its rightful ruler. As a returning king might set up his flag to rally his subjects to him after defeating the one who had taken over his realm, so Jesus speaks of a rallying point: But I, when I am lifted up from the earth, will draw all men to myself. Here is the banner Isaiah spoke of when he wrote, 'In that day the Root of Jesse will stand as a banner for the peoples; the nations will rally to him, and his place of rest will be glorious' (Isa 11:10). Here is the fulfillment of the messianic prophecies that the tribes of the earth will gather on Mt. Zion to worship God. But the gathering place is not the temple, for Jesus has replaced the temple. The one sacrifice on the cross will fulfill the function of the sacrifices of the temple, and in Jesus' own person (to myself) is the presence of God, whom they went to the temple to worship. The new community is grounded in the work of the cross."* Whitacre goes on to say, *"Satan, the jailer, has been mortally wounded, and Jesus, the liberator, is standing in the cell, but many prisoners prefer to remain in bondage!"*[11]

> *"His authority on earth allows us to dare to go to all the nations. His authority in heaven gives us our only hope of success. And His presence with us leaves us no other choice." ~ John Stott*

Jesus proclaims His absolute authority before He commissions His followers to go into the entire world with the life changing message of the Gospel. He knew His followers would face

---

[11] Whitacre, Rodney A. *John.* Vol. 4., Downers Grove, Ill: InterVarsity Press, 1999.

resistance from the enemy, but He wanted them to be assured that even though the enemy would indeed resist them, the devil would never be able to stop them from making disciples and establishing Kingdom realities upon the Earth, for ALL authority had been given to Him!

When you consider the fact that Jesus has all authority and has commissioned you to expand His Kingdom upon planet earth, what comes to your mind?

_____

_____

_____

_____

What does it truly mean to have ALL authority both in Heaven and upon earth?

_____

_____

_____

_____

How has the enemy tried to counter the authority of Jesus in your life?

_____

_____

_____

_____

Fullness Of The Holy Spirit

"And they were all filled with the Holy Spirit and began to speak with other tongues, as the Spirit was giving them utterance."   Acts 2:4 (NASB)

Up until the Day of Pentecost when the Church was birthed (which is recorded in the Book of Acts chapter two) the Spirit of God would only rest upon certain people, and with many of these people the Spirit would come and go, such as Samson. When Samson exerted feats of supernatural strength the Bible says the Spirit of God *"came upon him"*, but it didn't stay. There were prophets like Elijah and Elisha with whom it seems the Spirit of God actually stayed upon them. Still, with both cases the Spirit only rested on them, never did He take up residence inside of them.

On the Day of Pentecost when the Holy Spirit took up residence inside of the followers of Christ things changed forever. The Bible records this, saying, *"When the day of Pentecost had come, they were all together in one place. And suddenly from heaven there came a sound like the rush of a violent wind, and it filled the entire house where they were sitting. Divided tongues, as of fire, appeared among them, and a tongue rested on each of them. All of them were filled with the Holy Spirit and began to speak in other languages, as the Spirit gave them ability"* (Acts 2:1-4, NRSV). At this point the Spirit of God actually came to live inside the believer, the power of Heaven would now be with the followers of Christ everywhere they went! The followers of Christ now had the power of Christ to do the work of Christ, just like we do today!

This experience of being filled with the Holy Spirit is one that no prophet, king, or priest of the Old Testament had ever experienced!

God has purchased us with His very own blood, and now has taken up residence in the vessels which He has purchased! This is why the Apostle Paul told the church at Corinth, *"Or do you not know that your body is the temple of the Holy Spirit who is in you, whom you have from God, and you are not your own? For you were bought at a price; therefore glorify God in your body and in your spirit, which are God's"* (1 Corinthians 6:19-20, NKJ).

Paul also said, *"I have been crucified with Christ; and it is no longer I who live, but Christ lives in me; and the life which I now live in the flesh I live by faith in the Son of God, who loved me and gave Himself up for me"* (Galatians 2:20, NASB). Paul understood that the Spirit of Christ was not only abiding in him, but ready to express His will and power by wielding it through him! The Spirit of Christ was literally living through the Apostle Paul! This is the gift all believers have been given! We have an opportunity to allow the Spirit of Christ to live, not only in us, but through us!

"Since the days of Pentecost, has the whole church ever put aside every other work and waited upon Him for ten days, that the Spirit's power might be manifested? We give too much attention to method and machinery and resources, and too little to the source of power." ~ Hudson Taylor

The Spirit of Christ, which lives inside of us, is a source of power that God's people never had before the Book of Acts (at least not like we do now). When the adversary came against Job, he didn't have this source of power to resist the enemy! When we compare our circumstances to Job, or any other person in the Old Testament, we must understand that we have a source of power they never did! We have the Spirit that raised Jesus from the dead living inside of us!

Peter wrote, *"Be sober, be vigilant; because your adversary the devil walks about like a roaring lion, seeking whom he may devour"* (1 Peter 5:8, NKJ). The devil is loose upon this world, free to afflict all he can, causing destruction and mayhem throughout the world. But, we have a greater power that lives within us, a power that cannot be stopped and will not be denied! As representatives of Christ, with the Spirit of Christ living in us, we are to actively oppose Satan and his dark angels!

We have the power of Christ to do the work of Christ! *"The Son of God came to destroy the works of the devil"* (1 John 3:8, NLT). Jesus told His followers, *"I tell you the truth, anyone who believes in me will do the same works I have done, and even greater works, because I am going to be with the Father"* (John 14:12, NLT).

"The Church is the Body of Christ, and the Spirit is the Spirit of Christ. He fills the Body, directs its movements, controls its members, inspires its wisdom, supplies its strength. He guides into truth, sanctifies its agents, and empowers for witnessing. The Spirit has never abdicated His authority nor relegated His power." ~ Samuel Chadwick

The Spirit of Christ has fully equipped us to demolish the works of the devil, while at the same time establishing Kingdom realties, proclaiming the Gospel to the world, and making disciples of all mankind! If we can only grasp the power we have been given, and indeed the responsibility that goes along with that power, we will change the world for Christ, and there will be no person or devil that can stop us!

What does it mean to you to be filled with the Holy Spirit?

_____

_____

_____

_____

How should being filled with the Holy Spirit affect your life?

_____

_____

_____

_____

How has the Holy Spirit dwelling inside you affected the way you engage the enemy in battle?

_____

_____

_____

_____

Delegated Authority

"I will give you the keys of the kingdom of heaven; and whatever you bind on earth shall have been bound in heaven, and whatever you loose on earth shall have been loosed in heaven." Matthew 16:19 (NASB)

As Jesus traveled with His disciples to Caesarea Philippi He poses a question to them, asking, *"who do people say that I am?"* It is at this point that Peter confesses Jesus to be the Christ, the Son of the living God. It's also at that moment in Caesarea Philippi, of all places, that Jesus tells His followers, *"And I also say to you that you are Peter, and upon this rock I will build My church; and the gates of Hades will not overpower it. I will give you the keys of the kingdom of heaven; and whatever you bind on earth shall have been bound in heaven, and whatever you loose on earth shall have been loosed in heaven"* (Matthew 16:18-19, NASB). There has been much debate over the years to exactly what Jesus meant when He said these words, but a brief examination of the cultural understanding of the day about the gates of Hades will help us to better appreciate exactly what Jesus was trying to communicate to His followers then, and what He wants them to understand today.

It's no accident that Jesus makes His comments about the gates of hades and the keys of heaven at Caesarea Philippi. Caesarea Philippi sat at the foot of Mount Hermon, where the sons of God from Genesis chapter six made a covenant with each other to rebel against God and take for themselves wives of the daughters of men. Caesarea Philippi was the home of the Greco-Roman god Pan, whose imagery has helped to shape the modern persona that many hold of Satan with pointy ears, horns, a tail, and goat hooves and legs. But most importantly for our conversation, Caesarea Philippi was known as the gates of hades in the ancient world, and this is exactly cultural context from which these first century Jewish men who followed Jesus would have understood His comments.[12] Caesarea Philippi had a long history of great spiritual evil, and would have been viewed in many ways as the nerve center for the kingdom of darkness by the disciples.

When Jesus proclaimed at Caesarea Philippi that He was going to build His Church and the gates of Hades would not prevail against it, He was putting the forces of darkness on notice, and He was making it crystal clear to His followers that the war was on, and they were on the winning side. When Jesus gave the keys to the Kingdom to His followers, he was giving them

---

[12] G. del Olmo Lete, "Bashan," in Dictionary of Deities and Demons in the Bible, 2nd ed. (ed. Karel van der Toorn, Bob Becking, and Pieter W. van der Horst; Leiden; Boston; Cologne; Grand Rapids, MI; Cambridge: Brill; Eerdmans, 1999), 161-162.

Hamp, Douglas. "Did Jesus Thwart the Gates of Hades and the Underworld from Opening at Caesarea Philippi?". (2021).

authority over the forces of darkness. Authority He expected them to use, as they went forward proclaiming the Good News, destroying all the works of darkness, and establishing Kingdom realities. Keys throughout the Scriptures represent power and authority, and it's no different here. The followers of Christ have been given the authority and power of Heaven to represent the interest of Heaven here upon earth. It is for this reason Paul could say, *"So we are Christ's ambassadors; God is making his appeal through us. We speak for Christ when we plead, 'Come back to God'* (2 Corinthians 5:20, NLT)!

When we bind the spiritual forces of darkness we are at the same time loosening those who have been oppressed by the adversary. Binding and loosening happen at the same time. When the Apostle Paul encountered the demon possessed girl in Philippi and he commanded the demon to leave her, she was set free at the same time from the oppression the demon had brought to her life. The Book of Acts records the event, saying, *"One day, as we were going to the place of prayer, we met a slave-girl who had a spirit of divination and brought her owners a great deal of money by fortune-telling. While she followed Paul and us, she would cry out, 'These men are slaves of the Most High God, who proclaim to you a way of salvation.' She kept doing this for many days. But Paul, very much annoyed, turned and said to the spirit, 'I order you in the name of Jesus Christ to come out of her.' And it came out that very hour"* (Acts 16:16-18, NRSV). The demon was bound from the slave girl, and at the same time the slave girl was loosed from the oppression the demon brought to her life. As a representative of Jesus Christ you have the power and authority to bind the forces of darkness and loose those who are oppressed by them.

Sin, sickness, poverty, lies, and despair are all methods used by the forces of darkness to bring destruction to mankind. When looking forward to what Jesus would do for all of mankind who would put their trust in Him, Isaiah said, *"Surely he has borne our infirmities and carried our diseases; yet we accounted him stricken, struck down by God, and afflicted. But he was wounded for our transgressions, crushed for our iniquities; upon him was the punishment that made us whole, and by his bruises we are healed"* (Isaiah 53:4-5, NRSV).

God's will for mankind is good and pleasing! This is why the Apostle Paul wrote, *"Don't copy the behavior and customs of this world, but let God transform you into a new person by changing the way you think. Then you will learn to know God's will for you, which is good and pleasing and perfect"* (Romans 12:2, NLT). To experience this good, pleasing, and perfect will, in which the blessings of God are manifested in our lives, we must be set free from the lies of the enemy. Lies that tell us sickness and poverty are from God, and that God simply works in mysterious ways, and because of this people suffer such things. This simply is not true! Remember, if you believe the liar, you empower the liar! *"Christ has rescued us from the curse pronounced by the law. When he was hung on the cross, he took upon himself the curse for our wrongdoing. For it is written in the Scriptures, 'Cursed is everyone who is hung on a tree.' Through Christ Jesus, God has blessed the Gentiles with the same blessing he promised to Abraham, so that we who are believers might receive the promised Holy Spirit through faith"* (Galatians 3:134-14, NLT).

Jesus has all authority, and has delegated that authority to His followers to impose His will upon the Earth. The Church of Jesus Christ is the legal governing body in this world. *"For a child will be born to us, a son will be given to us; And the government will rest on His shoulders...There will be no end to the increase of His government or of peace, On the throne of David and over his kingdom, To establish it and to uphold it with justice and righteousness From then on and forevermore...*" Isaiah 9:6-7 (NASB).

Gates provide and image of a defensive weapon, they are designed to keep unwanted individuals out and to keep others in. So it is with the Gates of Hell imagery Jesus uses, they are an image of Satan's desire to keep the followers of Christ out of his business to wreak havoc and destruction upon the earth, and to keep the lost and suffering of this world trapped under his dominion. Jesus was clear that the Gates of Hell would not be able to withstand the Church. The church is not to be passive, but rather assertive and proactive in its efforts to bring the Gospel to the lost and to destroy all the works of the devil, such as poverty, sickness, hopelessness, and despair.

The local church is not meant to be a social club or an adult babysitting service, but a militant assembly of believers committed to making war against the devil, purposely and relentlessly advancing the Kingdom of God! William Booth, the founder of the Salvation Army, put it well when he said, "*We are not sent to minister to a congregation and be content if we keep things going. We are sent to make war and to stop short of nothing but the subjugation of the world to the sway of the Lord Jesus.*" Jesus was clear, the Gates of Hell cannot stop His followers who are armed with His power and authority, but if the enemy can find a way to keep us out of the war, not engaged in the affairs of our Lord, he has won a victory over us. Remember, "*No one serving in the army gets entangled in everyday affairs; the soldier's aim is to please the enlisting officer"* (2 Timothy 2:4, NRSV).

Much like a criminal who uses their power illegally to steal, kill, and destroy, so Satan and his dark angels illegally use their power against mankind to cause mayhem and destruction.

Only Jesus, and His Church which He has authorized, have legal status to use the power they've been given to establish Kingdom rule and realities!

> *"Government is not mere advice; it is authority, with power to enforce its laws."* ~ *George Washington*

We have been given legal authority from the King of kings to enforce and establish His will upon Earth, as it has already been done in Heaven!

It is important to consider, if we are going to wield the authority and power of Christ against the forces of darkness, we must remain subjected to that same power and authority. No story in the Scriptures demonstrates this truth better than that of the Roman Centurion who sought out the help of Jesus to heal his servant. Jesus was willing to help, and was ready to go to the Centurion's home, but the Centurion realized it was not necessary for Christ to come to his home, Jesus simply needed to give the word. Matthew records the incident in his account of the Gospel, saying, *"When he entered Capernaum, a centurion came to him, appealing to him and saying, "Lord, my servant is lying at home paralyzed, in terrible distress." And he said to him, 'I will come and cure him.' The centurion answered, 'Lord, I am not worthy to have you come under my roof; but only speak the word, and my servant will be healed. For I also am a man under authority, with soldiers under me;*

and I say to one, 'Go,' and he goes, and to another, 'Come,' and he comes, and to my slave, 'Do this,' and the slave does it.' When Jesus heard him, he was amazed and said to those who followed him, "Truly I tell you, in no one in Israel have I found such faith" (Matthew 8:5-10, NRSV).

Jesus was taken back by the Centurion's response, for he understood something that no one in Israel did. The Centurion understood that to exercise the authority and power of a governing system you had to be subject to that governing authority as well, for when you were submitted to that governing authority, all of its power and resources supported you and your works. The message is clear for the followers of Christ, if we expect to wield the authority and power of Heaven, we must be submitted to that same authority. We cannot expect to use the Key of Heaven if we are not willing to yield our lives and will to the ruler of Heaven. James helps us to understand this principle better when he says, *"Submit yourselves therefore to God. Resist the devil, and he will flee from you. Draw near to God, and he will draw near to you. Cleanse your hands, you sinners, and purify your hearts, you double-minded"* (James 4:7-8, NRSV). If you want to live in the authority and power of Heaven, destroying all the works of the adversary in your life and the world around you, stay submitted to God, for if you are not under His authority, you will not be able to exercise His authority over the powers of Hell.

Just as with the baptism of the Holy Spirit, we have been given a type of authority which no one in the Old Testament ever carried, with the exception of Adam before the Fall. Job never had authority over the adversary, but because Jesus took back the authority that was lost by Adam, and delegated it to us, we do!

Although the enemy has no authority upon this Earth, he continues to operate illegally. We must recognize his lack of authority to use his power, as we confront, and destroy, his works in the world around us!

> *"It is not that God is stingy and must be coaxed, for He 'giveth liberally and upbraideth not.' It is that we ourselves are so shallow and sinful that we need to tarry before Him until our restless natures can be stilled and the clamor of outside voices be deadened so that we can hear His voice. Such a state is not easily reached, and the men God uses have paid a price in wrestlings and prevailing prayer. But it is such men who rise from their knees confident of His power and go forth to speak with authority."* ~ Vance Havner

The more time we spend with God in prayer and through the Scriptures the more we will truly understand the ultimate authority of Christ, and the authority He has delegated to His Church to carry out His Great Mission!

Never forget, your King has ALL authority; meaning the enemy has none! Your King has delegated that authority to you, so begin to use His authority in the war (which as an enlisted soldier of Christ you are part of) against the spiritual forces of darkness!

The more we use our authority which Christ has given us, the more we will understand how to use it!

What is authority?

_____

_____

_____

_____

How can you exercise your delegated authority?

_____

_____

_____

_____

How does the enemy compensate for his lack of authority?

_____

_____

_____

_____

Delegated Power

"But you will receive power when the Holy Spirit comes on you; and you will be my witnesses in Jerusalem, and in all Judea and Samaria, and to the ends of the earth." Acts 1:8 (NIV)

As we have been delegated heavenly authority, so we have also been delegated heavenly power! We have been given the power of the Holy Spirit to enforce our authority, or rather our King's authority, upon Earth!

Much like a police officer's badge, which speaks to the authority they have been given, so the seal of the Holy Spirit testifies to the authority Christ has delegated to His followers. And, as a police officer possesses a host of weaponry to enforce their legal given authority, so we have been given power from the Holy Spirit to enforce the will of our King, and establish the realities of our Homeland in the world around us.

> *"The greatness of a man's power is the measure of his surrender."* ~ *William Booth*

We have been given the power of the Holy Spirit, but just as with the authority we've been given, learning to use that power takes practice and training.

If you were handed a gun and bullets, but didn't know how to load the gun, or correctly aim it and fire it at the target, the weapon would do you little good. So it is with the power of the Holy Spirit, we will need practice with this power, and help learning to use it from someone with practical experience; that means someone who has actually *"loaded the gun"* and *"fired at the enemy"*.

Just as there are criminals with varying strength and skill to cause havoc and destruction, so there are certain evil spirits that are stronger and more skilled at their evil works. Just as a police officer would call for reinforcements when facing a more dangerous criminal, there are times we must call for reinforcement from our brothers and sisters in Christ when facing strong spiritual forces.

We see this principle put into play by one of God's angels when confronting the evil spiritual prince who ruled over Persia. *"But for twenty-one days the spirit prince of the kingdom of Persia blocked my way. Then Michael, one of the archangels, came to help me, and I left him there with the spirit prince of the kingdom of Persia"* (Daniel 10:13, NIV). The angel called for Michael, who was stronger and more capable, to aid him in his struggle against this evil spirit.

There will be times when we need to call for help when facing the forces of darkness, and we must not hesitate to do so!

> *"All Christian power springs from communion with God and from the indwelling of divine grace." ~ James H. Aughey*

The devil lacks authority, but he still has power. We on the other hand have both authority and power, and the more we exercise them, the more adept we will be at using them to advance the Kingdom of our Lord, while destroying the works of Satan's dark kingdom!

Describe the power that has been delegated to you through the Holy Spirit?

_____

_____

_____

_____

Why have you been given this power? And why do you need
it?

_____

_____

_____

_____

Tell how you have exercised both the power and authority
you have been given to advance the Kingdom of God and
destroy the works of the devil in the past?

_____

_____

_____

_____

How could you more purposely and aggressively do this in
the future?

_____

_____

_____

_____

Chapter 11

Our Weapons

"We are human, but we don't wage war as humans do. We use God's mighty weapons, not worldly weapons, to knock down the strongholds of human reasoning and to destroy false arguments." 2 Corinthians 10:3-4 (NLT)

The war we are to wage against Satan and his dark kingdom is real! And though the weapons we are to fight with are not conventional earthy weapons, which are naturally thought of when you mention the word "*war*" they are just as real, and if used correctly and skillfully they are much more powerful than any gun or bomb.

Our outlook must be a spiritual one, understanding that spiritual realities determine physical realities. If we attempt to fight the world system which the enemy has established through mere physical means, we will be met not only with frustration, but certainly with failure as well!

The weapons we have been entrusted with carry the supernatural power of our Divine God! We must learn to depend on them as our weapons of choice to change our environment, while crushing the enemy at the same time!

> *"See the Gospel Church secure, And founded on a Rock! All her promises are sure; Her bulwarks who can shock? Count her every precious shrine; Tell, to after-ages tell, Fortified by power divine, The Church can never fail." ~ Charles Wesley*

155

If the Church of Jesus Christ will humbly rely on the power of Heaven, given to us by our Lord, we will be unstoppable! *"For every child of God defeats this evil world, and we achieve this victory through our faith. And who can win this battle against the world? Only those who believe that Jesus is the Son of God"* (1 John 5:4-5, NLT).

> *"We must not confide in the armour of God, but in the God of this armour, because all our weapons are only 'mighty through God.'"* ~ *William Gurnall*

The weapons we are to use in our warfare are mighty, capable of pulling down strongholds and destroying false arguments, because they are powered by the MIGHTY strength of our God!

Describe the method of warfare the Church is to use?

_____

_____

_____

_____

Describe the power which the Church is to engage the enemy with?

_____

_____

_____

_____

Why does so much of the Church seem to lack power?

_____

_____

_____

_____

How can this lack of power be overcome?

_____

_____

_____

_____

The Scriptures

"All Scripture is God-breathed and is useful for teaching, rebuking, correcting and training in righteousness, so that the servant of God may be thoroughly equipped for every good work." 2 Timothy 3:16-17 (NIV)

The Word of God is our most powerful weapon! The Bible compares the Word of God to a sword: *"the sword of the Spirit, which is the word of God"* (Ephesians 6:17, NKJV). The Word of God serves as a spiritual weapon, for we are fighting a spiritual battle! And the truth is, this spiritual battle affects everything in the physical world. So, if we want to change the physical world we must engage the spiritual forces around us!

The Word of God is a powerful two-edged sword that will never tarnish or rust, it will never grow dull or chip, it will remain forever sharp and powerful! It will continue to serve as a powerful weapon for the skilled soldier of Christ to wield against the forces of Darkness!

> *"The living Word is able to destroy satanic forces." ~ Smith Wigglesworth*

The Word of God is indeed able to destroy satanic powers, for it alone is what our Master used to fight off Satan when He was attacked in the wilderness. Three times Satan tried to tempt Jesus; to lure Him and His God given destiny to a place of destruction. And three times the Master skillfully swung the sword of the Spirit, destroying His adversary's onslaught! Matthew records the confrontation, saying, *"The tempter came and said to him, 'If you are the Son of God, command these stones to become loaves of bread.' But he answered, 'It is written, One does not live by bread alone, but by every word that comes from the mouth of God.' Then the devil took him to the holy city and placed him on the pinnacle of the temple, saying to him, 'If you are the Son of God, throw yourself down; for it is written, He will command his angels concerning you, and On their hands they will bear you up, so that you will not dash your foot against a stone.' Jesus said to him, 'Again it is written, Do not put the Lord your God to the test.' Again, the devil took him to a very high mountain and showed him all the kingdoms of the world and their splendor; and he said to him, 'All these I will give you, if you will fall down and worship me.' Jesus said to him, 'Away with you, Satan! for it is written, Worship the Lord your God, and serve only him.' Then the devil left him, and suddenly angels came and waited on him."* (Matthew 4:3-11, NRSV).

The Word of God, when used in faith, is a great weapon that the enemy cannot defend himself against! We must know without a doubt that God's Word is forever sure, and can never fail, regardless of the illusion the enemy may attempt to portray before our eyes!

Remember, the enemy is a master of deception, and uses his skillfully crafted lies to cause the children of God to doubt the Scriptures. When we doubt the Scriptures, we hold the sword of the Spirit loosely, and wield it carelessly, as we embrace the enemy's lies through human reasoning, making the Word of God of no effect! *"Making the word of God of no effect through your tradition which you have handed down. And many such things you do"* (Mark 7:13, NKJV).

> *"There are four things that we ought to do with the Word of God - admit it as the Word of God, commit it to our hearts and minds, submit to it, and transmit it to the world." ~ William Wilberforce*

By committing God's Word to our hearts, we can become skillful in using it, and will not be quickly deceived by the enemy's manipulation of it! By submitting to the Word, we move in faith, and it is faith that makes all things possible! As we communicate the Word to the world, and the demonic forces around us, we create Kingdom change that brings the Will of God to pass on Earth just as it does in Heaven!

Do you confess the Word of God out-loud? Why or why not?

_____

_____

_____

How much time do you spend daily committing God's Word to your heart's memory? Is it working? If not, what steps can you take to improve your efforts?

_____

_____

_____

_____

How should you use the Scriptures to fight off the attacks of the enemy, and secure victory?

_____

_____

_____

_____

Prayer

"Epaphras, who is one of you and a servant of Christ Jesus, sends greetings. He is always wrestling in prayer for you, that you may stand firm in all the will of God, mature and fully assured." Colossians 4:12 (NIV)

The battleground where we will meet and fight our enemy is entered onto through prayer!

Paul relays to the church in Colosse that Epaphras was wrestling in prayer for them. That is, Epaphras was engaging the enemy through prayer on their behalf.

Prayer is the vehicle we use to engage the enemy purposely and directly on the field of battle!

Prayer is a powerful ally for the soldier of Christ! The enemy has no concern over the child of God who doesn't pray! The devil knows that it is prayer which moves the hand of God! And that is something he truly fears, for he knows the power invoked when God's hand begins to move on behalf of His children! *"And this is the boldness we have in him, that if we ask anything according to his will, he hears us. And if we know that he hears us in whatever we ask, we know that we have obtained the requests made of him"* (1 John 5:14-15, NRSV).

> *"The one concern of the devil is to keep Christians from praying. He fears nothing from prayerless studies, prayerless work, and prayerless religion. He laughs at our toil, mocks at our wisdom, but trembles when we pray." ~ Samuel Chadwick*

The prayer of faith, which comes into agreement with heavenly realities, has the power to lay waste to all the enemy has built up!

Prayer recognizes the supreme power of Heaven, as it reaches up to God in faith, to release the power of Heaven into its earthly situations! *"The heartfelt and persistent prayer of a righteous man (believer) can accomplish much [when put into action and made effective by God—it is dynamic and can have tremendous power]"* (James 5:16, AMP).

"When the devil sees a man or woman who really believes in prayer, who knows how to pray, and who really does pray, and, above all, when he sees a whole church on its face before God in prayer, he trembles as much as he ever did, for he knows that his day in that church or community is at an end." ~ R. A. Torrey

If the enemy can keep the Church of Jesus Christ, which is made up of all believers around the world, ignorant to the power that is available to her when she falls before her Lord in prayer, he can keep the Church in bondage through his lying devices!

We must be deliberate in our prayers, as well as consistent, regardless of circumstance! We cannot afford to falter in our prayer life, or to enter there-in as a mere religious expression! We read in the Book of Acts of a time when Paul and Silas were arrested, beat, and imprisoned. Their solution was not to complain about their situation, nor did they simply give up, believing they had done all they could. NO! Instead they turned to the Lord in prayer and won the battle over the adversary. The Scriptures say, *"About midnight Paul and Silas were praying and singing hymns to God, and the prisoners were listening to them. Suddenly there was an earthquake, so violent that the foundations of the prison were shaken; and immediately all the doors were opened and everyone's chains were unfastened"* (Acts 16:25-26, NRSV). Prayer releases the power of God into our lives and trials, it gives us the ability to overcome all the works of the enemy (especially when its mixed with praise)! Prayer has the power to shake the foundations of hell and to break every chain! Do you want to live in the power of God, overcoming all the works of the adversary? Commit yourself to daily prayer and praise!

You should enter into prayer in faith, understanding the sheer power of it, and the absolute necessity of it in the war you are engaged in! You should enter in with great expectation of seeing God's hand moving in your life and in the world around you! You should enter in with an unwavering assurance of God's Word, rejecting the lies and illusion the enemy has placed before your eyes!

Describe the power prayer has to change the world?

_____

_____

_____

_____

Why does prayer carry such power?

_____

_____

_____

_____

How can you see your prayers become more powerful?

_____

_____

What strategies might the enemy use to keep you from praying?

_____

_____

_____

_____

What steps can you take to shield yourself from these strategies?

_____

_____

_____

_____

Our Testimony

"And they overcame and conquered him because of the blood of the Lamb and because of the word of their testimony, for they did not love their life and renounce their faith even when faced with death." Revelation 12:11 (AMP)

The word of our testimony is a powerful weapon when it comes to doing battle with the enemy!

The word used here for testimony in the Greek is *marturia* which carries the meaning to give a report or to produce evidence of some subject matter. Most interesting is the fact that *marturia* is derived from the Greek word *martus* which Jesus used when He told His followers that they would be a witness unto Him throughout all the Earth (Acts 1:8).

So, we find that when we are a witness to others of all Jesus has done for us, it serves as a weapon to buffet the lying-destructive works of the enemy!

Our words carry power, and when they are baring record of the goodness of God that we have received through Jesus Christ, they are capable of producing unimaginable results in our struggle against Satan and his cohorts!

We are reminded of the incredible power of our words to guide the direction of our life by James when he writes, *"We can make a large horse go wherever we want by means of a small bit in its mouth. And a small rudder makes a huge ship turn wherever the pilot chooses to go, even though the winds are strong. In the same way, the tongue is a small thing that makes grand speeches..."* (James 3:3-5, NLT).

We have the power to change the tide when the devil attacks us, regardless of what area of our life it may be by speaking out the testimonies the Lord has given us! When we give witness to others of the Lord's goodness and mercy, it's like beating the devil in the head with a large sledgehammer!

> *"The best thing for the saint to do is to claim the victorious name of the Lord Jesus over every onslaught of the enemy." ~ Watchman Nee*

We must make a habit of speaking out loud to others the many testimonies we have recorded in our hearts and minds of the wonderful and miraculous things our Father in Heaven has done for us through, and because of, Jesus Christ our Lord! Our attitude should reflect that of the psalmist, when he said, "*My life is an example to many, because you have been my strength and protection. That is why I can never stop praising you; I declare your glory all day long*" (Psalms 71:7-8, NLT).

> *"We ought to take as great care about the words we speak as we do about the fruit of our trees or the increase of the earth, which we are to eat; for, according as they are wholesome or unwholesome, so will the pleasure or the pain be wherewith we shall be filled." ~ Simon Patrick*

The enemy loves to entice us to speak words of destruction and doubt, forgetting how the Lord saved us, and how He has blessed us so many times since that day! He rejoices when we embrace his temptations to speak words of death and destruction into our lives and the trials we face. For he knows the power of those words, and longs to see us forget the testimonies of the Lord, so that we may never speak of them again! Never forget how good God has been to you! "*Let all that I am praise the LORD; with my whole heart, I will praise his holy name. Let all that I am praise the LORD; may I never forget the good things he does for me. He forgives all my sins and heals all my diseases. He redeems me from death and crowns me with love and tender mercies. He fills my life with good things. My youth is renewed like the eagle's"* (Psalms 103:1-5, NLT)!

Understand clearly, *"Words kill, words give life; they're either poison or fruit—you choose"* (Proverbs 18:21, MSG). If you want to put to ruin the plans and attacks of the enemy, speak out loud the testimonies of the Lord! Share with all who will listen how God has blessed you and prospered you! Talk of the great mercy and the saving grace you have received through Jesus Christ! Speak words that give life!

Describe a testimony in your own words?

_____

_____

_____

_____

Why is a testimony so powerful when countering the attacks of the enemy?

_____

_____

_____

_____

How, and why, do the words that proceed from your mouth have such a profound effect on your life?

_____

_____

_____

_____

Chapter 12

Our Significance

"Dear friends, we are already God's children, but he has not yet shown us what we will be like when Christ appears. But we do know that we will be like him, for we will see him as he really is" (1 John 3:2, NLT).

The depth of our existence should not be overlooked because of the material world we live in. It is a world system that has been constructed by the evil one, and it consistently attempts to cover-up who we are as the children of God. Heed the warning of the Apostle John when he wrote, *"Do not love this world nor the things it offers you, for when you love the world, you do not have the love of the Father in you. For the world offers only a craving for physical pleasure, a craving for everything we see, and pride in our achievements and possessions. These are not from the Father, but are from this world. And this world is fading away, along with everything that people crave. But anyone who does what pleases God will live forever"* (1 John 2:15-17, NLT). The Scriptures declare that *"He raised us from the dead along with Christ and seated us with him in the heavenly realms because we are united with Christ Jesus"* (Ephesians 2:6, NLT). We have been given a life of power, privilege, and responsibility as God's children, called to represent His interest in the battle between the forces of darkness and the forces of light. Paul gives us a glimpse of what we shall one day become when he says, *"Don't you realize that someday we believers will judge the world? And since you are going to judge the world, can't you decide even these little things among yourselves? Don't you realize that we will judge angels? So you should surely be able to resolve ordinary disputes in this life*" (1 Corinthians 6:2-3, NLT). John likewise gives us a glimpse into the greatness and privilege that awaits us when he writes, "*Then I saw thrones, and the people sitting on them had been given the authority to judge. And I saw the souls of those who had been beheaded for their testimony about Jesus and for proclaiming the word of God. They had not worshiped the beast or his statue, nor accepted his mark on their foreheads or their hands. They all came to life again, and they reigned with Christ for a thousand years*" (Revelation 20:4, NLT).

Jesus will eventually return to carry out the final conviction upon the forces of evil. Paul reminds us of this when he writes, "*Then comes the end, when he hands over the kingdom to God the Father, after he has destroyed every ruler and every authority and power. For he must reign until he has put all his enemies under his feet. The last enemy to be destroyed is death*" (1 Corinthians 15:24-26). But, until that day comes we have a responsibility to go forth destroying all the works of the adversary and expanding the family of our God by sharing the hope of the Gospel that all His children carry.

Our Responsibility

"But when people keep on sinning, it shows that they belong to the devil, who has been sinning since the beginning. But the Son of God came to destroy the works of the devil." 1 John 3:8 (NLT)

Jesus came to destroy the works of the devil, and as you go forth proclaiming the truth of the Gospel message, you can be certain you will be confronted by the demonic forces of darkness and their destructive works. As a representative of Christ, sent out into the world system, you carry the responsibility to progress the Mission of Christ by destroying the works of the devil and establishing Kingdom realities as you advance the Kingdom, proclaiming the glorious message of the Gospel!

> *"The need today is for a company of overcoming saints who know how to wage war for the release of those under the enemy's deception." ~ Watchman Nee*

Perhaps nowhere else in the Bible can we find a better parallel of our Mission, as it corresponds to Christ, then in the Book of Esther; specifically, in chapter eight, when the Jewish people face annihilation because of the evil and deceptive plot of Haman.

> "On that day King Ahasuerus gave Queen Esther the house of Haman, the enemy of the Jews. And Mordecai came before the king, for Esther had told how he was related to her. So the king took off his signet ring, which he had taken from Haman, and gave it to Mordecai; and Esther appointed Mordecai over the house of Haman. Now Esther spoke again to the king, fell down at his feet, and implored him with tears to counteract the evil of Haman the Agagite, and the scheme which he had devised against the Jews. And the king held out the golden scepter toward Esther. So, Esther arose and stood before the king, and said, 'If it pleases the king, and if I have found favor in his sight and the thing seems right to the king and I am pleasing in his eyes, let it be written to revoke the letters devised by Haman, the son of Hammedatha the Agagite, which he wrote to annihilate the Jews who are in all the king's provinces.

For how can I endure to see the evil that will come to my people? Or how can I endure to see the destruction of my countrymen?' Then King Ahasuerus said to Queen Esther and Mordecai the Jew, 'Indeed, I have given Esther the house of Haman, and they have hanged him on the gallows because he tried to lay his hand on the Jews. You yourselves write a decree concerning the Jews, as you please, in the king's name, and seal it with the king's signet ring; for whatever is written in the king's name and sealed with the king's signet ring no one can revoke.' So the king's scribes were called at that time, in the third month, which is the month of Sivan, on the twenty-third day; and it was written, according to all that Mordecai commanded, to the Jews, the satraps, the governors, and the princes of the provinces from India to Ethiopia, one hundred and twenty-seven provinces in all, to every province in its own script, to every people in their own language, and to the Jews in their own script and language. And he wrote in the name of King Ahasuerus, sealed it with the king's signet ring, and sent letters by couriers on horseback, riding on royal horses bred from swift steeds" (Esther 8:1-10, NKJV).

There are at least seven truths we can take from this passage about the responsibility we have been given by our King to destroy the works of the devil and advance the Kingdom of our God.

1. We Have The King's Signet.

"So the king took off his signet ring, which he had taken from Haman, and gave it to Mordecai; and Esther

appointed Mordecai over the house of Haman" (Esther 8:2, NKJ).

> ➤ The ring was the seal of the king. Any order that was given by the king had to have his seal, and once the order was sealed it was official and had to be carried out. Giving this ring to Mordecai was giving him the power to act as the king. Mordecai could give any order at this point, and once sealed with the signet it would have the same power as an order given by the king himself.

> ➤ Our King has given us His name and Spirit that we may represent Him with the exact same authority and power that He has, right here, right now, upon this Earth!

"These miraculous signs will accompany those who believe: They will cast out demons in my name, and they will speak in new languages. They will be able to handle snakes with safety, and if they drink anything poisonous, it won't hurt them. They will be able to place their hands on the sick, and they will be healed" (Mark 16:17-18, NLT).

2. Partnered With The King To Do His Will.

"You yourselves write a decree concerning the Jews, as you please, in the king's name, and seal it with the king's signet ring..." (Esther 8:8, NKJ).

> ➤ King Ahasuerus made his will concerning the Jews known to Esther and Mordecai, but he left it up to Mordecai to carry out that will the way he saw fit. The king had done his part to save the Jews, the rest was up to Mordecai; their fate was now in his hands.

> ➤ Jesus has done very much the same thing with us. He has given us His Will through His Word and now allows us to carry out His Will in varying ways. God allows us to use our imagination and special giftings in fulfilling the Great Commission. Jesus has done His part to save mankind on the cross, now the rest is up to us. The fate of the lost and oppressed of mankind is now in the hands of the followers of Christ.

> ➤ An imagination doesn't have to be a bad thing or an evil thing. An imagination focused on Jesus and His Mission, which is under the guidance of the Holy Spirit, is a powerful tool for the advancement of God's Kingdom!

"God will do this, for he is faithful to do what he says, and he has invited you into partnership with his Son, Jesus Christ our Lord" (1 Corinthians 1:9, NLT).

3. An Order That Cannot Be Revoked.

"… for whatever is written in the king's name and sealed with the king's signet ring no one can revoke" (Esther 8:8, NKJ).

➢ When Mordecai gave an order sealing it with the king's signet ring that order was all powerful, and could not be revoked! Mordecai understood the power he now possessed to save the Jews!

➢ We must understand the power we have been given! When we give an order here on this Earth in the name of our King Jesus, in the power of the Holy Spirit, by which we have been sealed, that lines up with the MISSION we have been called to, that order is all powerful and cannot be revoked.

"So will My word be which goes forth from My mouth; It will not return to Me empty, Without accomplishing what I desire, And without succeeding in the matter for which I sent it" (Isaiah 55:11, NASB).

4. The Order Must Be Given.

"So the king's scribes were called at that time, in the third month, which is the month of Sivan, on the twenty-third day; and it was written, according to all that Mordecai commanded, to the Jews, the satraps, the governors, and the princes of the provinces from India to Ethiopia, one hundred and twenty-seven provinces in all, to every province in its own script, to every people in their own language, and to the Jews in their own script and language" (Esther 8:9, NKJ).

➤ For the king's will to be done Mordecai was going to have to actually give the order. Without the order actually being given nothing would have happened!

➤ We have been given authority and power to fulfill the Great Commission and destroy the devil's work, but we must give the order! We must speak the words! We must come into agreement with heavenly realities through prayer here on Earth, believing in faith that our prayers will produce great fruit for the Kingdom of our God!

"And this is the boldness we have in him, that if we ask anything according to his will, he hears us. And if we know that he hears us in whatever we ask, we know that we have obtained the requests made of him." (1 John 5:14-15, NRSV). Jesus also assures His followers, *"If you abide in me, and my words abide in you, ask for whatever you wish, and it will be done for you. My Father is glorified by this, that you bear much fruit and become my disciples"* (John 15:7-8, NRSV).

5. An Order In The King's Name.

"And he wrote in the name of King Ahasuerus…" (Esther 8:10, NKJ).

➤ King Ahasuerus had great power and those who represented his name shared that power.

➤ We represent the name of our King Jesus and that name is ALL powerful. We have great power when we operate in His name!

"You haven't done this before. Ask, using my name, and you will receive, and you will have abundant joy" (John 16:24, NLT). Never forget who you represent, for His name is above all names and He is ruler over all! *"Christ is the visible image of the invisible God. He existed before anything was created and is supreme over all creation, for through him God created everything in the heavenly realms and on earth. He made the things we can see and the things we can't see—such as thrones, kingdoms, rulers, and authorities in the unseen world. Everything was created through him and for him. He existed before anything else, and he holds all creation together"* (Colossian 1:15-17, NLT).

6. Sealed With The King's Signet.

*"**sealed it with the king's signet ring**..."* (Esther 8:8, NKJ).

➤ There were always those who tried to use the king's authority who had not been given the right. The order that was sealed by the signet was known to be from the king and therefore carried all his power and authority.

➤ A word spoken in the name of Jesus must carry His seal, which is none other than the Holy Spirit!

➢ For the name to carry power in the spiritual and physical realm, the one using the name must have the King's seal, His signet ring, which is the Holy Spirit. The Holy Spirit gives the order power! *"In Him you also trusted, after you heard the word of truth, the gospel of your salvation; in whom also, having believed, you were sealed with the Holy Spirit of promise"* (Ephesians 1:13, NKJ).

7. The Order Must Be Sent.

*"...**and sent letters by couriers on horseback, riding on royal horses bred from swift steeds**"* (Esther 8:10, NKJ).

➢ The order once given in the name of the king and sealed with his signet would have done no good if it stayed in Mordecai's hands. It had to be sent.

➢ When we give an order in the name of our King and it is sealed by the power of the Holy Spirit, it must be sent if it is to do any good. Mordecai sent the order he gave by horseback; we send the orders we give in the name of our King by faith!

➢ Faith is the horse and rider that carries the commands we give, so that they may become a reality! Faith makes all things possible! Faith is the very electricity in the phone line when we make a call to heaven! Without faith, our prayers

178

and words mean nothing, and have no chance of accomplishing anything in the spiritual realm, which means they will never be manifested in the physical realm; they are worthless! When you make your request known to the Lord, or you speak out a word in the name of the Lord, you must have faith!

"Truly I tell you, if you say to this mountain, 'Be taken up and thrown into the sea,' and if you do not doubt in your heart, but believe that what you say will come to pass, it will be done for you. So I tell you, whatever you ask for in prayer, believe that you have received it, and it will be yours" (Mark 11:23-24, NRSV). Remember, *"Faith is the assurance of things hoped for, the conviction of things not seen...By faith we understand that the worlds were prepared by the word of God, so that what is seen was made from things that are not visible"* (Hebrews 11:1-3, NRSV).

How will you begin to more purposely fulfill the great responsibility given to you by your King?

_____

_____

_____

_____

What are the consequences of ignoring the responsibility given to you by your King?

_____

_____

_____

_____

*"Finally, **be strong in the Lord and in the strength of his power**. Put on the whole armor of God, so that you may be able to stand against the wiles of the devil. For our struggle is not against enemies of blood and flesh, but against the rulers, against the authorities, against the cosmic powers of this present darkness, against the spiritual forces of evil in the heavenly places. Therefore take up the whole armor of God, so that you may be able to withstand on that evil day, and having done everything, to stand firm. Stand therefore, and fasten the belt of truth around your waist, and put on the breastplate of righteousness. As shoes for your feet put on whatever will make you ready to proclaim the gospel of peace. With all of these, take the shield of faith, with which you will be able to quench all the flaming arrows of the evil one. Take the helmet of salvation, and the sword of the Spirit, which is the word of God"*
(Ephesians 6:10-17, NRSV).

Made in the USA
Columbia, SC
07 October 2024

43172874R00112